Critical Issues in Infant-Toddler Language Development

Designed to help students and educators make critical theory-to-practice connections, this essential volume provides a deep yet accessible approach to infant and toddler language and literacy education. Centered around four foundational topics—language, interaction, and play; language and culture; multilingualism; and early literacy—each section starts with a chapter breaking down the research and theory, followed by two practice chapters, from both leadership and teacher perspectives, that illustrate key concepts across a range of infant-toddler contexts. Ideal for students in early language and literacy courses as well as programs on infant-toddler development, this critical resource helps readers thoughtfully and practically bring multilingual and multiliterate development to the infant and toddler years.

Daniel R. Meier is Professor of Elementary Education at San Francisco State University, USA, and has written widely on young children's language and literacy learning.

Critical Issues in Infant-Toddler Language Development

Connecting Theory to Practice

Edited by
Daniel R. Meier

Routledge
Taylor & Francis Group

NEW YORK AND LONDON

Cover image: Shutterstock

First published 2023
by Routledge
605 Third Avenue, New York, NY 10158

and by Routledge
4 Park Square, Milton Park, Abingdon, Oxon OX14 4RN

Routledge is an imprint of the Taylor & Francis Group, an informa business

Library of Congress Cataloging-in-Publication Data
A catalog record for this title has been requested

ISBN: 978-1-032-13133-7 (hbk)
ISBN: 978-1-032-13065-1 (pbk)
ISBN: 978-1-003-22781-6 (ebk)

DOI: 10.4324/9781003227816

Typeset in Sabon
by Taylor & Francis Books

In memory of Jasper Wu, Alan Kurdi, and Jace Young. May their memories be a blessing for all young children everywhere.

Contents

Figures

Tables

Contributors

Nodelyn Abayan is a doctoral candidate at San Francisco State University in Educational Leadership and Social Justice. She holds an MA in Education with a concentration in Early Childhood Education from the same university. She is currently the Infant-Toddler Program Coordinator at the Early Childhood Education Center at San Francisco State University. Nodelyn has worked for close to two decades in the ECE field. She has been a Mentor Coach, an Education Manager, an adjunct professor at City College of San Francisco and San Francisco State University, and was an Infant Toddler teacher for 6 years.

Iliana Alanís, a native of South Texas, is a Professor of Early Childhood and Elementary Education in the Department of Interdisciplinary Learning and Teaching for the University of Texas at San Antonio. As a university faculty member, she engages teacher candidates and practicing teachers for their work in culturally and linguistically diverse classrooms with a primary focus on the rights of young children to develop their native language and cultural identity. Dr. Alanís uses a sociocultural lens to examine effective pedagogical practices in early childhood, dual language contexts.

Emily Bugos holds an MA in Education with a concentration in Early Childhood Education. Emily previously worked as an infant/toddler teacher at the Associated Students Early Childhood Education Center and currently works as the Child Development Program Manager at North Marin Community Services overseeing the early childhood education and school age childcare programs. She is a former infant/toddler caregiver, PITC certified trainer, and holds a Child Development Site Supervisor permit. Emily also works as a lecturer at San Francisco State University in the Elementary Education department and as a consultant for Early Care Educators of San Francisco.

Annick De Houwer is Director of the Harmonious Bilingualism Network (HaBilNet; www.habilnet.org). She was trained in linguistics and socio- and psycholinguistics at several Belgian universities and at Stanford University (the latter on a Fulbright scholarship). She obtained her doctorate in Linguistics from the Free University of Brussels in 1988. She held professorial positions at the universities of Antwerp and Brussels in Belgium and at the University of Erfurt in Germany, where prior to becoming Professor Emerita she held a professorship in Language Acquisition and Multilingualism. De Houwer's research has mainly focused on bilingual and monolingual children's language development. She has served as series editor of *Trends in Language Acquisition Research* and *IMPACT: Studies of Language in Society* (for John Benjamins) and has co-edited several books, most recently *The Cambridge Handbook of Bilingualism* (for Cambridge University Press, with Lourdes Ortega). She is the author of *The Acquisition of Two Languages from Birth: A Case Study, Bilingual First Language*

Acquisition, An Introduction to Bilingual Development, and *Bilingual Development in Childhood*. She has served in various professional organizations such as the International Association of Applied Linguistics (AILA). She is currently (2021–2024) the President of the International Association for the Study of Child Language (IASCL). Annick leads an international and multilingual life and aims to spend the next few years helping bilingual families so they may experience Harmonious Bilingualism.

Cheryl Horney is the Program Director at an early Head Start/Head Start Program in San Francisco, CA. She has a Bachelor's degree from Boston University and a Master's in Education from San Francisco State University. She has worked with infants, toddlers and preschoolers for nearly two decades. She serves on the executive committee of the San Francisco Child Care Planning Advisory Council and the Board of Directors of Lotus Bloom Family Resource Center in Oakland, CA. She is the proud mother of a young son.

Iheoma U. Iruka, PhD, is a Research Professor in the Department of Public Policy, a Fellow at the Frank Porter Graham Child Development Institute (FPG), and the Founding Director of the Equity Research Action Coalition at FPG at the University of North Carolina at Chapel Hill. Dr. Iruka is leading projects and initiatives focused on ensuring that minoritized children and children from low-income households start of well, such as through family engagement and support, quality rating and improvement systems, and early care and education system and programs. Dr. Iruka focuses on ensuring excellence for young diverse learners, especially Black children and their families, through the intersection of anti-bias, anti-racist, culturally grounded research, program, and policy.

Daniel R. Meier is Professor of Elementary Education at San Francisco State University. His research focuses on early childhood language and literacy development, teacher inquiry and reflection, teacher professional growth, and international education. Meier has written widely on early childhood education, and is the author, most recently, of *Supporting Literacies for Children of Color: A Strength-Based Approach to Preschool Literacy Education* (Routledge, 2020), and a co-author of *Learning Stories and Teacher Inquiry Groups: Reimagining Teaching and Assessment in Early Childhood Education* (NAEYC, 2021). His current research projects focus on teacher inquiry groups as early childhood professional development, and the use of memoir for understanding children's identities and family histories.

Azul Muller holds an MA in Education with a concentration in Early Childhood Education. Azul currently serves as Preschool Mentor Teacher at the Felton Institute, Early Care and Education Programs in San Francisco. Previously, Azul was an early childhood educator in preschool and infant/toddler classrooms. Azul is passionate about preserving and honoring children's languages, developing experiences to help children develop a strong identity, and fostering reflective practice with teachers she mentors.

Seferina Rivera is a second-generation San Franciscan native of Jewish and Mexican descent. She is currently the Infant Toddler Head Teacher at Mills College Children's School, where she has been teaching for the last 20 years. She also serves as a mentor teacher for Mills undergraduate and graduate students pursuing their degrees in Early Childhood Education. She has been teaching infants and toddlers since 1990. She holds a BA in Child Development from Humboldt State University with a minor in Ethnic Studies. She also holds an MA in ECE from Mills College. Her focus of interest is attachment theory, documentation, and infant mental health.

Haneefah Shuaibe-Peters has worked in the field of early education for over 17 years. She holds a Masters in Early Childhood Education and a Doctorate in Educational Leadership from San Francisco State University. She has an extensive background in leading ECE programs, parent education and community college instruction. She currently serves as the Executive Director for two large non-profit childcare facilities in the San Francisco Bay Area for children 0-6 years of age. As a lecturer at several Bay Area community colleges, she focuses on building teachers' confidence and critical thinking skills. Her specialty areas include infant/toddler growth and development, kindergarten readiness, childcare environments, family supports and early intervention. As a wife and mother of three, she is most passionate about providing ECE professionals and family service providers with practical tools for improving and enriching the lives of families and children.

Mariana Souto-Manning, PhD, became Erikson's 5th President in September 2021. Mariana has served as professor of education at Teachers College, Columbia University and held additional academic appointments at the University of Iceland and King's College London. Committed to the pursuit of justice in early childhood teaching and teacher education, Mariana's research centers the lives, values, and experiences of intersectionally minoritized people of Color. An Afro-Latina first-generation immigrant, Mariana earned her bachelor's, master's, and PhD at the University of Georgia, after having started her higher education journey at Dekalb Community College. Mariana has (co-)authored 10 books, dozens of book chapters, and over 80 peer-reviewed articles. She has received a number of research awards, including the American Educational Research Association Division K Innovations in Research on Diversity in Teacher Education Award.

Patricia Sullivan holds an MA and EDD in early childhood education. She's also the owner and director of Baby Steps, a home-based childcare program in San Francisco. She is a veteran early childhood educator, highly experienced with inquiry, reflection, antiracist education, and language and literacy teaching. She is a passionate advocate for equity and social justice in early childhood education, and her research publications have focused on instructional and institutional supports for African-American children and families, nature education, and narrative and critical literacy.

Crystasany R. Turner is an Assistant Professor in teacher education at Erikson Institute in Chicago, IL. Her teaching and research focus includes early childhood education for social justice, culturally responsive and sustaining pedagogy, and Black feminist epistemologies. She has authored numerous articles and book chapters that interrogate imbalanced social power, institutional inequities, and systemic oppression affecting diverse children and families. Her scholarship has been published in *Urban Education, Journal of Urban Learning, Teaching and Research*, and the *Early Childhood Exchange* among others.

Jennifer M. Ventura is a bilingual Spanish and English speaker with 18 years of experience in early childhood education. She has had the opportunity to work in various capacities with diverse communities in the Bay Area. She has worked as an ECE educator, Early childhood interventionist, Developmental Inclusion coach, Instructional coach, and trainer. Her expertise includes facilitating professional learning communities, coaching, and training on different child development topics focusing on ages birth to five. Jennifer holds a BA in Child and Adolescent Development with a concentration in Young Child and Families, a Master's degree in Education with a focus on Early childhood, and a certificate in Inclusive Early Childhood Practices from San Francisco State University.

Acknowledgements

I thank all of the amazing contributors to this volume on infant and toddlers' language and literacy learning—Nodelyn Abayan, Iliana Alanís, Emily Bugos, Annick De Houwer, Cheryl Horney, Iheoma U. Iruka, Azul Muller, Seferina Rivera, Haneefah Shuaibe-Peters, Mariana Souto-Manning, Pat Sullivan, Crystasany Turner, and Jennifer Ventura. They all believed in this project and contributed their chapters amid Covid and their busy personal and professional lives. I have only worked previously with one of the contributors to this volume, so it was exciting and a joy for me to collaborate with so many new colleagues on this book. These contributors represent a highly experienced, knowledgeable, and passionate group of researchers and educators dedicated to improving the social, cultural, and educational lives of our very youngest children and their families. Now more than ever, we need these kinds of perspectives and words of wisdom from veteran early childhood researchers and educators, so a huge thank you to each of you for contributing your important chapters. I also thank the editorial and production team at Routledge for their support and guidance; it's always a pleasure to work with them on another project. I also wish to acknowledge Larissa Hsia-Wong, who provided invaluable research assistance for the book, as well as Tania Renee Durden, Amber Friesen, Mina Kim, Ben Mardell, Yue-Ting Siu, and Gloria Quiñones for reviewing some of the material. Thanks, finally, to the children and families who appear in this book—as always, there is no book on early childhood without real children and families.

Introduction

Daniel R. Meier

Opening Reflections

1   What are your major personal and professional goals for reading this book on infant and toddler language and literacy learning?
2   What are your plans for taking notes and reflecting on the research, theory, and practical strategies described and discussed in this book?

Whenever I feel nostalgic for when my children, Kaili and Toby, were infants and toddlers, I search for my collection of several pads of long yellow legal paper, and my set of audio and videotapes. From when Kaili (now age 24) and Toby (now age 17) were newborns until about age 7 or 8, I wrote down the sounds and communicative efforts of their first whispering, chortling, crying, cooing, and then their babbling, singing, words, phrases, and sentences. I also audiotaped and videotaped their language, and when I now replay the tapes, I can hear and see again the power of their earliest language, its movement, beauty, energy, and purpose.

For example, here is a brief audiotape excerpt of three-month-old Kaili's language and communication as she lay on her changing table:

> Kaili's slow cry starts low in tone and then quickly rises in pitch and urgency to a small crescendo. Then comes a slightly longer stretch of much softer crying interspersed with hard breathing. This then switches to a stretch of more crying though in a staccato style with a consistent rhythm: /da duh/, /da duh/, /da duh/, which is then followed by more crying at a slightly faster rate and with a new rhythm: /ah uh/, /ah uh/, /ah uh/ and Kaili cries at a faster and faster rate as she sounds more and more agitated (as if Kaili were essentially saying, "Dad, pay attention and pick me up!").

In a set of snippets of Toby's language, here is a chronological, developmental sampling of what I documented for Toby's oral language from birth through 30 months:

0–6 months:
crying, cooing, smiling, gazing, pointing, gesturing

6–12 months:
babbling

DOI: 10.4324/9781003227816-1

14 months:
mah-mah
dah dah
bay-bee

20 months:
Granpa
Granma
I brang it.
I seed it.
Sand in there (i.e. truck).
Balloon pop.
Make noise.

26 months:
I'm scared of the deer.
Don't fall.
'pecial beads.
Make a ramp!
Daddy, don't read.

30 months:
When I was a baby, I used to crawl.
Trader Joe's makes it. (i.e. the cheese)
Do teenagers like cough drops?
Can I get a fruit rollup?
Where are them? (i.e. his shoes)

Whether we are novice or veteran early childhood educators, we know that the first few years of life are foundational for the multilingual and multiliteracy learning of young children in the early childhood years and beyond. When infants and toddlers are afforded access to languages and literacies in a range of supportive social, cultural, and educational contexts, they start their education from a strengths-based foundation. The infant and toddler years, though, are not simply a preparation ground, a readiness stage, for pre-school and beyond. Children's lives from birth through age 3 are critical years in and of themselves, where children feel, observe, engage, and problem-solve the languages and literacies that matter to them, their families, communities, and teachers. As infants and toddlers move and watch and absorb the sounds and movements of their environments, they immerse themselves in an ever-evolving set of puzzles and wonders of their own creation and volition:

- What are my caregivers communicating to me through their warmth of touch and the timbre and tone of their voices?
- How can I respond to changes in sound, movement, light, and color?
- What actions and gestures can I take to learn about my new world?
- What actions and gestures help me get noticed by others?
- What sounds in my environment do I need to pay attention to?
- What sounds can I make, and what can these sounds do for me in the here-and-now?
- Who is speaking to me, and what kinds of languages am I hearing?
- How are people expecting me to interact with them verbally and nonverbally?

- Which elements of the literacies, images, and symbols in my world help me engage with others?
- How can languages and literacies affirm the social and cultural traditions and values of my family and community?

To anticipate and support children's language and literacy needs and talents, young children need empowered, knowledgeable, and socially and politically aware families, teachers, administrators, and other early childhood professionals to understand and support children's 0–3 language and literacy growth.

Infants and toddlers also need families and educators who are aware of the disempowering effects of racism in society and in education, and who work against racism in all forms to support the development and learning of all infants and toddlers of Color over their lifetimes. Ample research, for instance, has shown that the first 1000 days of life are critical for the well-being of African American children, their families, and their communities, and infant and toddler educators are key change agents in promoting anti-racist and culturally responsive 0–3 early education (Iruka et al., 2021).

This book, then, affirms the central role of all educators in uncovering the power and beauty of languages and literacies for infants and toddlers and their families in a range of learning contexts. To this end, this book is divided into four major areas that form the foundation for children's language learning:

- language, interaction, and play;
- language and culture;
- multilingualism; and
- early literacy.

The opening chapters in each of the major sections are written by language and literacy researchers who discuss critical theory and research and offer implications for practice and teaching. The opening theory and research chapters are then followed by two chapters written by veteran infant-toddler teachers and administrators who offer specific approaches, ideas, and strategies for implementing selected aspects of language and literacy theory and research. All of the chapters are original and have not appeared in any other publication. The chapters were written specifically to address critical ideas and strategies in each of the four major parts, and taken as a whole they constitute a comprehensive theory-to-practice call to action for strengthening infant and toddler language and literacy education.

Language, Interaction, and Play

Infants and toddlers learn languages and literacies when they are immersed in warm, intimate playful social interactions with peers, siblings, parents, extended family, and community members. Daily interactions with others motivate young children to watch and listen and learn from others and to observe nuances of sound, light, movement, and human intention in their early environments. Play, in all of its manifestations and in concert with other humans and objects, is the foundation for children's interactions and communicative exchanges for objects, peers, educators, and family members.

> Play is impressive in its variety. Typically, it is guided by the subjective aspirations of its participants and because of that assumes shapes that are quite transient and fragile. It can present meanings that operate at different levels and in different ways. But

> I maintain that play displays particular overriding qualities that make it different from other behaviors. To some extent, play expresses a general pattern of human relating.
>
> (Henricks, 2018, p. 137)

The chapters in this opening section address questions and challenges for integrating language, play, and social interaction:

- How can we validate and recognize infants and toddlers as highly capable and competent inquirers, problem solvers, and conversational partners?
- What are effective ways that infant-toddler administrators and leaders can organize and structure children's play and interaction to promote early communication and language learning?
- What are successful strategies for teachers to conceptualize and create learning environments to support meaningful social connections and early language development?

In Chapter 1, I discuss key theory and research dimensions for understanding how and why children use and learn language through play and social interaction. In Chapter 2, Nodelyn Abayan, an infant-toddler program coordinator for a campus-based center, describes leadership goals and strategies for promoting social interaction to enhance children's language learning. In Chapter 3, Emily Bugos, an infant/toddler teacher and Nodelyn's colleague, discusses specific ways to establish indoor and outdoor spaces for infants-toddler language growth.

Language and Culture

Infants and toddlers become engaged in language and literacies through immersion in the cultural and social environments of home, community, and education. These cultural and social influences are founded upon the traditions, worldviews, and values passed down and cherished over generations in families and communities. In turn, these influences influence the forms and functions of the languages and literacies that children are exposed to and socialized into by families, communities, and educators.

> Each individual belongs to multiple social and cultural groups. This creates richly varied and complex social identities (related to race, gender, culture, language, ability and disability, and indigenous heritage identities, among others). Children learn the socially constructed meanings of these identities early in life, in part by recognizing how they and others who share or do not share them are treated. Early childhood educators and early childhood programs in centers, homes, and schools play a critical role in fostering children's development of positive social identities.
>
> (National Association for the Education of Young Children, 2019, p. 13)

The chapters in this second section address key processes in linking languages and culture in infant-toddler literacy education:

- What roles do varied sociocultural traditions and contexts play in protecting and preserving children's language learning and growth?
- How can educators adopt a critical stance toward infant and toddler language and literacy learning that is anti-racist, equitable, and inclusive for children and families?
- How can educators recognize and support the language and literacy needs and talents of children with disabilities and their families?

In Chapter 4, Dr. Iliana Alanís, Professor of Early Childhood/Elementary Education at the University Texas at San Antonio, and Dr. Iheoma Iruka, Research Professor in the Department of Public Policy, University of North Carolina at Chapel Hill, outline foundational theory and research on social and cultural contexts for children's language development in varied cultural contexts. In Chapter 5, Dr. Patricia Sullivan, longtime owner/director of a family child care program and teacher educator, describes her vision and approach for creating anti-racist language and literacy opportunities starting in infancy. In Chapter 5, Jennifer Ventura, a developmental inclusion specialist with First5 San Francisco, focuses on practical ideas and assessment approaches for supporting the language development of children with disabilities.

Multilingualism

In the US and globally, multilingualism is a preferred and necessary goal for those families and educators seeking to maintain cross-border connections with loved ones and opportunities for travel and work. Yet the US early childhood system continues to lack cohesive multilingual policies in centers, programs, and schools, and so early childhood educators fashion their own local approaches to maintain and expand multilingual opportunities for infants and toddlers.

> The greatest challenge I see is helping infant and toddler practitioners honor and value the multiple languages, literacies, and cultural knowledge that our infants and toddlers bring with them to the classroom. Much of our early childhood curriculum, policies, and best practices are rooted in individualist culture and monolingual practices that do not allow opportunities for practitioners to intentionally and effectively build upon and include the experiences and knowledge of ethnically and linguistically diverse children.
>
> (R. R. Durden, personal communication, November 13, 2021)

The chapters in this third section, then, highlight key issues and questions for conceptualizing and nurturing children's multilingual development:

- How and why can young children become bilingual, and what are important influences as well as challenges?
- How can we support families to promote multilingualism at home and also in educational settings?
- How can we strengthen environmental and instructional supports for multilingual learning, and how can we support our colleagues in this process?

In Chapter 7, Dr. Annick De Houwer, Professor Emerita, University of Erfurt, Germany, and Director of the Harmonious Bilingual Network in Europe, presents critical research and theory examining powerful ways for children to become multilingual in US and other international settings. In Chapter 8, Azul Muller, a Spanish/English infant, toddler, and preschool educator at the Felton Institute, San Francisco, discusses effective strategies to support young children and families' cultural and language growth in bilingual classrooms. In Chapter 9, Seferina Rivera, an infant-toddler educator at the Mills College Children's School, Oakland, offers her vision and approach for supporting multilingualism for infants, toddlers, and families in an English-medium classroom.

Early Literacy

Early literacy is increasingly seen as an integral component of infant and toddler programs and curricular approaches, and foundational for children's later success in preschool, the primary grades, and beyond. Children's successful introduction to early literacy hinges upon thoughtful and engaging curricular and interactional approaches that provide a strengths-based vision for early literacy learning.

> A strength-based approach also takes into account the literacy memories, beliefs, and goals of children's families and the full range of their home, community, and educational contexts. As early childhood educators, we play a pivotal role in shaping and enacting an engaging literacy curriculum that connects ourselves to children as literacy consumers and creators. This educational vision is also political, as a strength-based literacy education necessitates investing in the social, cultural, and intellectual capital and resources of young children of Color, and ensuring their educational success and achievement as preschool and lifelong learners
>
> (Meier, 2020, p. xvi)

The chapters in this final section emphasize critical issues and strategies for children's successful and meaningful early literacy development:

- What are foundational ideas for promoting a strengths-based, inclusive approach for all children's early literacy engagement and learning?
- What are effective strategies for supporting infants' and toddlers' earliest exploration of books and other forms of print?
- What are effective strategies for promoting children's creative and artistic engagement as a form of expression, communication, and identity?

In Chapter 10, Dr. Mariana Souto-Manning, President and Irving and Neison Harris President's Chair, Erikson Institute, and Dr. Crystasany Turner, Assistant Professor, Erickson Institute, outline central research and theoretical principles underlying a strengths-based approach for early literacy learning in home, community, and educational settings. In Chapter 11, Cheryl Horney, Head Start Director at Wu Yee Children's Services, San Francisco, discusses strategies for supporting children's engagement with multilingual children's books. In Chapter 12, Dr. Haneefah Shuaibe-Peters, the director of two preschools in Berkeley, California, describes her approach to promoting young children's artistic expression based upon her roles as a parent, teacher, and administrator.

Early Childhood Contexts, Children, and Families

The book's chapters describe meaningful language and literacy learning for infants and toddlers in a range of educational contexts—private independent programs, university campus-based childcare programs, small family childcare settings, and small and large public infant/toddler programs. The social and educational contexts portrayed in the book also vary in terms of racial and economic backgrounds, educational philosophies, curricular and assessment approaches, learning environments, teaching team structures, professional development opportunities, and forms of family outreach and engagement.

For instance, Patricia Sullivan's family childcare, featured in Chapter 5, is housed in Patricia's home which is adjacent to a large city park. Patricia interacts and talks with infants sitting or moving on her back porch, while at the same time Patricia can observe the older children running and playing just outside her backyard at the edge of the park. Patricia also works with a small group of teaching assistants, and they collaborate on a curriculum that emphasizes emergent learning, children's spontaneous and evolving interests, and anti-racist education. Patricia's program also values the professional development process of teacher inquiry, documentation, and reflection, as Patricia and her colleagues collect and discuss photographs, notes, and observations of children's language learning and growth.

The book also features educators, children, and families immersed in a range of languages, cultural backgrounds, and play and social contexts. The families represent varied structures and constellations, immigration and transnational histories and realities, perspectives on language learning and socialization, and knowledge of the traditional discourse patterns and educational approaches in schools.

For example, as discussed in Chapter 8, the children at Azul Muller's center are primarily children of Latina/o descent, with a small percentage of children of Asian American and African American heritage. Azul's site is part of her agency's administration of a total of four centers in San Francisco serving over 350 children and families. The agency also serves children with autism and medically fragile children, operates a teen pregnancy and wellness program, and provides food and nutrition for children and vocational services for families. The organization, then, provides a range of holistic, "wrap-around" services that nurture and support the multiple medical, nutritional, and educational talents and needs of children and families.

A Note to Readers

This book is primarily written for educators taking courses in infant and toddler development, children's language and literacy learning, and early childhood curriculum and administration at the college and university level. It is designed for both novice and experienced early childhood educators, including lead teachers, assistant teachers, administrators, coaches and mentors, inclusion specialists, family liaisons, and other early childhood professionals. The book also works well for early childhood educators participating in ongoing professional development at their worksite, as well as for educators participating in book clubs, professional learning communities, and teacher inquiry groups.

The book also highlights a number of key elements of infant and toddler language and literacy learning, which range from oral language to multilingualism to assessment (Table 0.1).

I encourage all readers to bring their own knowledge base—from life experiences, from college and university education, and also on-site professional development—to their individual and collective reading and reflecting on the value of this book for understanding and supporting the language and literacy learning of infants and toddlers. As you all know, those who work with infants and toddlers take on particular challenges as they provide an educational and moral contribution to well-being of our educational system and society. Their roles have become only more critical during the ongoing Covid-19 pandemic, as many families and communities depend on infant and toddler programs for safety, care, and learning. Finally, the contributors and I hope that the ideas and practices featured in this book resonate with you and invigorate your practice and professional growth, and support your lifelong journey in supporting young children's language and literacy learning.

Table 0.1 Key language and literacy elements discussed most prominently by chapter

Key Elements \ Chapters	1	2	3	4	5	6	7	8	9	10	11	12
Oral Language	•	•	•	•	•	•	•	•	•	•	•	•
Nonverbal Language	•	•	•	•	•	•	•	•	•	•	•	•
Play	•	•	•	•	•	•	•	•	•	•	•	•
Cultural and Social Interaction	•	•	•	•	•	•	•	•	•	•	•	•
Multilingualism	•	•		•	•	•	•	•		•		•
Anti-Racism & Education for Freedom	•		•	•					•			•
Early Literacy	•		•		•				•	•	•	•
Families	•		•			•	•	•		•	•	•
Assessment		•				•		•	•		•	
Teacher Inquiry and Reflection	•	•	•			•	•		•	•		•

Closing Reflections

1 Now that you've read this introduction, have your goals and purposes for reading this book changed? If so, how?
2 In looking at Table 0.1 again, place a check next to those elements that you have some knowledge about, place a star next to those elements that you would like to learn more about, and then take notes on these elements as you read and reflect on the rest of this book.

References

Henricks, T. S. (2018). Theme and variation: Arranging play's forms, functions, and colors. *American Journal of Play*, 10(2), 133–167.

Iruka, I. U., Durden, T. R., Gardner-Neblett, N., Ibekwe-Okafor, N., Sansbury, A., & Telfer, N. A. (2021). Attending to the adversity of racism against young Black children. *Policy Insights from the Behavioral and Brain Sciences*, 8(2), 175–182.

Meier, D. R. (2020). *Supporting literacy for children of color: A strength-based approach to preschool literacy*. Routledge.

National Association for the Education of Young Children. (2019). *Advancing equity in early childhood education: A position statement of the National Association for the Education of Young Children*. National Association for the Education of Young Children.

Part I

Language, Interaction, and Play

1 Language, Play, and Social Interaction

Key Dimensions

Daniel R. Meier

Opening Reflections

1 What do you believe are the core elements of effective language and literacy education for infants and toddlers?
2 Within this perspective, what do you see as key connections between language, play, and social interaction for infants and toddlers?

In this chapter, I discuss key research and theoretical dimensions underlying the inter-relationships between language, play, and social interaction for infants and toddlers. These dimensions apply to the full range of all young children's talents, abilities, interests, and passion for language, play, and interaction. All children play, all children interact socially, and all children use some form of language for communication, social and cultural engagement and inclusion, and identity development.

The developmental and cultural course of young children's language and literacy learning is influenced even before birth by the perceptions, values, and goals of family and community members for children as important conversants and participants in local language and literacy practices. Language, then, is always embedded in social and cultural values and practices, whether in homes or communities or educational settings, and from birth young children are motivated to use language in the service of increasing social and cultural inclusion and identity formation. As Geneva Smitherman (2006) so aptly notes, "Language is the tie that binds" (p. 3)—language is the glue that holds together the totality of young children's evolving social, cultural, intellectual, physical, and artistic development.

Language, the Human Body, and the Senses

From birth, infants are eager to engage with their senses and seek out patterns of inter-action, play, comfort, joy, and trust with individuals and objects in their immediate environments. Their eyes search for light and shadows that intrigue and delight; their ears listen for sounds and voices that soothe and comfort; their hands and fingers grasp objects for warmth and connection; and their whole bodies ease into being cradled, held, or carried for a sense of calm, safety, and belonging.

Key Idea

Their eyes search for light and shadows that intrigue and delight; their ears listen for sounds and voices that soothe and comfort; their hands and fingers grasp objects for

DOI: 10.4324/9781003227816-3

warmth and connection; and their whole bodies ease into being cradled, held, or carried for a sense of calm, safety, and belonging.

This comforting physical base allows children to experience and engage with changes in the environment. For example, when I held our first child, Kaili, as a newborn to see the sunshine through a window in our house each morning, the sunlight continually changed. One moment the sunshine dappled through the leaves of the oak tree in our backyard as it entered the room where I stood, the next moment the sunshine jumped with a sudden gust of wind, and then moved again as the sun brightened with the full parting of the clouds. As the sunlight changed in intensity and brightness both outside and inside the room, Kaili's eyes widened or she squinted or closed her eyes. And when I turned Kaili to look at the sunshine from a new angle or pulled back the curtain to block some light, Kaili's eye movements indicated that she registered these changes in light and brightness.

Children's physical development, then, is connected with rapid changes in children's capacity and desire for linking play, interaction, and language according to their individual desires, talents, and needs. While children vary in the rate of these physical and sensory connections, many children do follow certain patterns of development (King, 2007). As children become more active and capable physically, their physical movements become more intertwined with their nonverbal and oral language communication (Table 1.1).

Over time, as infants feel increasingly safe and secure, and increase their range of movement and ability to grasp objects, these objects play increasingly important roles in their language, play, and interactions. Sylvia Kind has noticed the power of objects and materials:

> Materials *live* in the world in multiple ways. They can evoke memories, narrate stories, invite actions, and communicate meanings. Materials and objects create meeting places ... Materials are not immutable, passive, or lifeless until the moment we *do* something to them; they participate in our early childhood projects. They live, speak, gesture, and call to us.
>
> (Kind, 2014, p. 865)

While some objects are beyond the developmental reach of infants and young toddlers, Kind's idea that "materials *live* in multiple ways" and that they are "not immutable, passive, or lifeless until the moment we *do* something to them," reminds us that young children use objects as developmental, social, and cultural bridges to connect key moments in evolving language growth, play, and interaction.

We can see the inter-twining of these language-play-interaction opportunities in the powerful story of "The Watch's Tick-Tock" from *The Diary of Laura* (Edwards & Rinaldi, 2008), where one-year-old Laura is captivated by her teacher Eluccia's watch. The scene starts as Laura looks at images in a printed catalogue and stares intently at a row of watches. Eluccia says, "These are watches," and shows Laura the watch on her wrist, and puts it close to Laura's ear "so she can hear the tick-tock." Laura listens "for a long time, intent, then she moves her ear away, pulls her head up, goes back to the images, stares at them again, and then with confidence, puts her ear next to the page" (p. 51). Laura moves from the printed page, to Eluccia, to the watch, and then back again to the page. The interplay between the watches on the page and the actual physical watch motivates Laura's back-and-forth, playful sensory movement, her nonverbal communication, and her social interaction with Eluccia.

Table 1.1 Infant physical development and language growth

Age	Physical Development	Language Growth
1 month	• Little movement, some head tilting	• Cries at loud noises • Quiets when listening to gentle speech
2 months	• Increased head lifting • Eyes follow objects	• Cries, smiles, gurgles, grunts
3 months	• On stomach, props up on forearms and lifts head and chest	• Cooing sounds • Recognizes and responds to familiar voices
4 months	• Increased head control • Can sit when propped up	• Increased cooing, squealing, gurgling noises • Repeats some sounds
5 months	• Brings feet and hands and mouth while lying on back • Rolls from stomach to back	• Coos and laughs • Increased attention to voices and sounds
6 months	• Roll from back to front and then back again • Plays with feet while lying on back • Reach for objects while on stomach	• Continued cooing and gurgling • Says "no" and makes other sounds to express emotions
7 months	• Pivots on stomach and crawls • Sits independently	• Initiates speech and approximates sounds like "mama mama" • Increased babbling and gesturing
8 months	• Reaches for toys while sitting • Early crawling • Pulls up to standing position	• Responds to their name • Increased babbling • Increased nonverbal communication
9 months	• Can move while standing and holding onto furniture • Increased crawling • Grasps objects between thumb and index fingertip	• Recognizes others' names • Responds to simple words • Increased sound and word imitation • Says "up" while raising arms
10 months	• Walks with one hand for balance on furniture • Extends wrist for grasping objects	• Calls or shouts for attention • More complex babbling • Enjoys music, rhymes, and games like "pat a cake"
11 months	• Plays in kneeling position • Sits with legs straight out • Holds objects with thumb and first two fingers	• Engages in "conversation" with others • Points to objects when asked • Responds to requests such as "give me the ball"
12 months	• Might try to walk alone • No arm swing when walking, requires total concentration	• Might produce first recognizable words • Babbles in what sound like sentences, "sounds as if he is engaging in conversation" • Nods or shakes head for yes or no

Source: King (2007, pp. 85–89)

The expansion of children's circle of play partners and interlocutors, then, goes hand in hand with their increased capacity for oral and nonverbal communication. Opportunities for play, interaction, and conversational partners nurture infants and toddlers' motivation for looking and listening for the nuances of movement and sound—both the familiar and the new.

> Their [infants] perceptual system is prepared in advance for processing language sounds. But infants are not only brilliant listeners. Although speech is not yet at their disposal, they are nonetheless preparing themselves for this moment by sharpening their vocal capabilities, organizing their perceptual abilities, and conversing with adults through looks, sounds, and gestures.
>
> (de Boysson-Bardies, 2001, p. 35)

Over time, this increasingly sophisticated preparation for speech and nonverbal communication coincides with physiological changes in children's acoustical capabilities—the "development of articulatory control takes time" as it is "a matter of governing the machine as a whole (tongue, lips, pharynx, larynx)" (de Boysson-Bardies, 2001, p. 17). The gradual production of children's speech is the "most complex motor activity that any person acquires," and speech production is closely connected to breath control, which allows children "to shape and control sound" (Leiberman, 2010).

As children cry, scream, coo, gurgle, babble, sing, mimic sounds and words, and then attempt to produce words on their own, children experiment with and tinker with the acoustic and sensory parameters of the languages in their environment. In doing so, children become attuned to the particular prosody, rhythm, pitch, intensity, and tones of the languages in their homes and communities, as well as to the individual timbre of the voices and the emotional resonance of their conversational, play, and interactional partners. For these reasons, we can intentionally support the language gifts of infants through lullabies, songs, rhymes, and stories early in life. For example, Ana Faleschini, a Spanish/English bilingual educator, wanted to expose her daughter, Bella, to the sounds of her language even before Bella was born:

> It was important for me to start utilizing singing, talking, story reading, and telling to support my baby's bilingual development. This preparation continued to the day she was born. The day she made her appearance into this world I did not know what to say, it was difficult to find the right words to use, instead of words I decided to make our first connection through the power of a song—"The Itsy Bitsy Spider" in Spanish. When Bella heard the familiar melody, the tune seemed to be immediately recognized.
>
> (A. Faleschini, personal communication, November 28, 2021)

This attention to the sounds of languages, as coupled with secure social bonds and cultural cohesion, support the gradual evolution of speech for infants and toddlers. Older infants and toddlers can gain a sense of pleasure in their earliest speech production, playing with vowels as musical sounds and learning to recognize and produce syllables as bounded acoustic entities. They derive particular satisfaction in producing repeated patterns, such as canonical babbling as in the repeated sounds of /ba/ba/ba/, and producing other babbling patterns as in /pa/ba/ma/ and /ma/ma/buh/. Often, at one year of age, children begin to recognize the specific language patterns and variations that give them the most joy and communicative power, and which prepare them for the satisfying process of producing pseudo and conventional words. Moving at their own rate along this developmental path, "the training of their articulatory capacities has given them the faculty to choose the rhythmic and syllabic frame that will furnish the bases for the articulatory programming of their first words" (de Boysson-Bardies, 2001, p. 51).

Play and Social Interaction

Play and social interaction are key partners for children's language development from birth. As Odegaard and Hedegaard (2020) point out, "Exploration by young children is central to their development as persons. To explore is a play-related action—a social situation that affects what and how objects or relations are explored" (p. 5). Within their ongoing exploration, the overall glue holding language, play, and interaction together involves "children's engagement and joy in exploration and curiosity, as well as under-standings, knowledge and skills" that "create meaningful competencies and life experiences" (Odegaard & Hedegaard, 2020, p. 5).

Play—Forms and Functions

Ample research helps us create a working typology of how children's play and language are intertwined over time (Table 1.2).

From birth through age 5, children engage with and move through a range of play forms that suit their momentary mood, their evolving personalities, the social overtures and cultural values of peers and adults, and the objects and materials of interest. As educators, we can use these play forms for understanding how and why children might pick and choose their favorite modes of play, mix and match these forms according to their personal interests and talents, and connect them with their local sociocultural play and language practices.

Playfulness and a Pedagogy of Play

A critical dimension to meet children where they are in their play development in com-bination with social interaction and language, involves our intentional efforts to define a "pedagogy of play" and "playful learning" (Mardell et al., 2016). A pedagogy of play is "a systematic approach to the practice of playful learning and teaching" (p. 2) and playful-ness is "the disposition to frame and reframe a situation to include possibilities for enjoyment, exploration and choice" (p. 3).

> **Key Idea**
>
> Playfulness is seen as "the disposition to frame and reframe a situation to include possibilities for enjoyment, exploration and choice" (Mardell et al., 2016, p. 3).

In this perspective, playful learning features three key inter-connected elements: choice, wonder, and delight. When choice is part of children's playful learning, children feel a sense of empowerment and autonomy; when wonder is involved in their playful learning, children experience curiosity, surprise, and challenge; and when their playful learning involves delight, children feel excited, satisfied, and a sense of belonging (Mardell et al., 2016).

A pedagogy of play provides an overall framework for connect language, play, and social interaction in our curriculum, observations and assessments, and interactions with

Table 1.2 Linking forms and functions of play with language development from birth to age 5

0–2 years	**Attuned, Exploratory, Object, and Small-Motor Play**	
	Play: Children's exploration, manipulation, and visual inspection of objects either independently or with others; can include possible use of objects as tools as well connections with symbolic play for older children (Bjorklund & Gardiner, 2011; Chang & Deák, 2019; Gordon, 2014)	*Language:* Pleasurable sounds and early word approximations accompany sharing and playful exchange of objects; adult-led games with objects and body movements feature songs and rhymes
	Solitary Play	
	Play: Preference for playing alone, can be linked with shyness and other individual preferences, though it is not exclusive of social play with others (Coplan et al., 2014)	*Language:* Sound effects, pleasurable noises, and even singing to accompany children's playful movements and object manipulation and experimentation
2–3 years	**Independent and Onlooker Play** (Gardner-Neblett et al., 2016)	
	Play: Play and exploration by oneself in varied play areas and with a range of objects, toys, books, instruments; children might play in close proximity to peers and adults; pausing to observe the play actions of others	*Language:* Turning the body to observe peers at play, facial expressions in response to observing peers; sound effects and pleasurable noises can accompany object manipulation
	Parallel Play	
	Play: Children playing on their own alongside or in close physical proximity with peers and adults (Majorano et al., 2015)	*Language:* Some turning of the body to observe nearby peers at play, facial expressions in response to observations of peers; possible handing of toys and objects to share or take with nonverbal and verbal expression
	Locomotor, Physical Activity Play, Rough and Tumble Play, Large-Motor Play	
	Play: Use of the human body and objects to increase motor activity and physical routines, can involve make-believe and symbolic play (Pellegrini, 2009; Tannock, 2011)	*Language:* Sound effects, words and phrases to accompany actions, repeated actions accompanied by language
	Imaginative, Pretend, Fantasy, Socio-Dramatic and Make-Believe	
	Play: Creating imaginary objects and situations, acting out roles such as from stories and books (Bodrova & Leong, 2015; Pellegrini, 2009; Vygotsky & Cole, 1978)	*Language:* Words, phrases, sentences using the language of pretense; language for silly and goofy interactions and some co-construction of play scenes
3–5 years	**Symbolic Play** (Closely linked with pretend and make-believe play)	
	Play: Children's engagement in pretense, and playful interactions with objects whereby children indicate that objects can represent multiple things (Meins et al., 2013, p. 1799)	*Language:* Words, phrases, sentences using the language of pretense; language to represent objects as tools and ideas; language to direct and cooperate with peers
	Guided Play, Games, and Playful Learning	
	Play: Supporting children's play via physical interaction and language; older children, youth, and adults can play varied guiding roles (Mardell et al., 2016; Tsao, 2008)	*Language:* Words, phrases, sentences to link action with roles and rules for both invented and established games; language to represent objects as tools; language to direct peers as well as cooperate

infants and toddlers. The idea of playfulness attunes our inquiry, documentation, and reflection skills to discover key moments and strategies for supporting children's language, play, and interaction.

Our Roles

Educators and families can take on a variety of roles to support a pedagogy of play and children's playfulness. In Chapters 2 and 3 of this book, for instance, colleagues Nodelyn Abayan and Emily Bugos respectively provide examples of how the continuity of care model offers children a stable group of peers and teachers over a multi-year span. This structure allows educators to become familiar with children's play and interactional preferences and styles, and to fine-tune our goals, materials, activities, and strategies for linking playful learning and a pedagogy of play (Mardell et al., 2016). In this long-term process, educators can assume a range of roles that include stage manager (organizing play environments), planner (creating scripts or routines for play), scribe (writing down children's words in play), mediator (supports children to brainstorm solutions to social challenges arising in play); player (teachers taking active roles in children's play); and assessor and communicator (learning to see the value and meaning of children's play) (Jones & Reynolds, 2015).

> **Our Roles in Supporting Children's Play**
>
> - Stage manager
> - Planner
> - Scribe
> - Mediator
> - Player
> - Assessor and communicator
>
>   (Jones & Reynolds, 2015)

Understanding the forms and functions of these play roles for adults in children's play involves close observation and time for reflection (Quiñones, Li, & Ridgway, 2021). Of particular importance is "when educators understand where children are coming from," which deepens educators' knowledge and skill in becoming "active play partners in play" (G. Quiñones, personal communication, November 11, 2021). Further, when educators "act as conversational partners," they help "develop children's language, but for this a close relationship needs to be developed, and for that time and space are needed" (G. Quiñones, personal communication, November 11, 2021). This is where the professional development process of inquiry, documentation, and reflection (as highlighted in several chapters in this book) provides a collaborative forum for understanding the benefits and limits of our play roles.

In addition to these play roles, we can also increase our awareness of play's "organizing principle" (Brown, 2008) and creation of "imaginatively created series of interconnected cortical play maps" (Sutton-Smith, 1981, as cited in Brown, 2008, p. 91) for helping children find their way socially, culturally, and linguistically as they construct their reality and identity. These play maps provide infants and toddlers with cognitive-based routes for meaningful language use and social interaction. Infants and toddlers also use play to organize their emerging identities and roles, as they seek out patterns of nonverbal and oral language in their immediate worlds (Maguire-Fong, 2014). In this way, we can see and support infants and toddlers as "active seekers" and "organizers" of information who are also "researchers who construct knowledge about the world they encounter" (Maguire-Fong, 2014, p. 5).

> **Key Idea**
>
> Infants and toddlers are active seekers, organizers, and researchers who construct knowledge about the world they encounter (Maguire-Fong, 2014, p. 5).

Child language research conducted 40 years ago revealed that children excitedly enter nonverbal and oral interactions with others through scaffolded interactions (Ninio & Bruner, 1978; Snow, 1977) and conversational interactions that resemble proto-conversations and turn-taking. Subsequent research has provided evidence of sociocultural influences on language and literacy practices that preserve cultural, familial, and communal beliefs and practices (González et al., 2006; Gregory, 2008; Heath, 1983; Nsamenang, 2005; Perry & Delpit, 1998; Rogoff et al., 2018; Smitherman, 2006; Souto-Manning, 2010).

As discussed in several chapters of this book, family and community members socialize infants and toddlers into language and literacy patterns and practices based upon time-honored cultural, social, and spiritual beliefs and values. These beliefs and values influence how children are supported in their knowledge construction and learning how to socialize and use critical forms and functions of language. In this book, several contributors highlight specific language-based practices that strengthen children's use of language for social and cultural inclusion—scaffolding, co-construction, showing, modeling, narrating, responding, playing, storying, and turn-taking.

These specific practices for adults, youth, and children come to life "in the endeavors of their communities, in a process of *transformation of participation*" (Rogoff et al., 2018, p. 7). In a simultaneous, multi-directional exchange of language, play, and social interaction, "people do not simply participate. They participate IN some event … and they are IN that process, along with their companions, building on ways of life of prior generations of their cultural communities" (p. 7).

Moving Forward

Our critical challenge, then, becomes rethinking how we conceptualize, plan, and contextualize our strategies for linking language, play, and socialization to understand and support the language learning of all children in all educational settings. A crucial element in this theory-to-practice transformation involves deepening our awareness of the danger of imposing a primarily Western view of learning and development on every language and learning context. This tradition in Western child development and education too often neglects and dismisses "local wisdom and situated intelligences" and "patterns of knowledge construction and human differentiation" (Nsamenang, 2005, p. 279).

> **Key Idea**
>
> This tradition in Western child development and education too often neglects and dismisses "local wisdom and situated intelligences" and "patterns of knowledge construction and human differentiation" (Nsamenang, 2005, p. 279).

What is needed, then, is a long-term view of educators' own knowledge construction of the array of beneficial supports for linking language, play, and interaction, and to spend our collective energy intentionally adopting and adapting strategies and practices to support all children in all learning contexts. This is what the remaining chapters in this book provide for us—theories and practices to deepen our knowledge and sharpen our practices for transforming infant-toddler language development for all children in all educational contexts.

Closing Reflections

1   How has this chapter provided new ideas, research, and theory for linking language, play, and interaction for infants and toddlers?
2   In looking again at Table 1.2, which forms of play are you most familiar with, and which forms would you like to learn more about? Which of the connections between play forms and language learning would you also like to learn more about?

References

Bjorklund, F., & Gardiner, A. K. (2011). Object play and tool use: Developmental and evolutionary perspectives. In A. D. Pellegrini (Ed.), *The Oxford handbook of the development of play* (pp. 153–171). Oxford University Press.

Bodrova, E., & Leong, D. J. (2015). Vygotskian and post-Vygotskian views on children's play. *American Journal of Play*, 7(3), 371–388.

Brown, S. (2008). Play as an organizing principle: Clinical evidence, personal observations. In E. Goodenough (Ed.), *A place to play: A companion volume to the Michigan television film: Where do the children play?* (pp. 83–98). National Institute for Play. doi:10.3998/mpub.362097.

Chang, L. M., & Deák, G. O. (2019). Maternal discourse continuity and infants' actions organize 12-month-olds' language exposure during object play. *Developmental Science*, 22(3), e12770.

Coplan, R. J., Ooi, L. L., Rose-Krasnor, L., & Nocita, G. (2014). "I want to play alone": Assessment and correlates of self-reported preference for solitary play in young children. *Infant and Child Development*, 23(3), 229–238.

de Boysson-Bardies, B. (2001). *How language comes to children: From birth to two years*. MIT Press.

Eddowes, E. A. (1991). Review of research: The benefits of solitary play. *Dimensions*, 20(1), 31–34.

Edwards, C., & Rinaldi, C. (2008). *The diary of Laura: Perspectives on a Reggio Emilia diary*. Redleaf Press.

Fleer, M. (2016). Theorising digital play: A cultural-historical conceptualisation of children's engagement in imaginary digital situations. *International Research in Early Childhood Education*, 7(2), 75–90.

Gardner-Neblett, N., Holochwost, S. J., Gallagher, K. C., Iruka, I. U., Odom, S. L., & Pungello, E. P. (2016). *Guided versus independent play: Which better sustains attention among infants and toddlers?* Society for Research on Educational Effectiveness.

González, N., Moll, L. C., & Amanti, C. (Eds.). (2006). *Funds of knowledge: Theorizing practices in households, communities, and classrooms*. Routledge.

Gordon, G. (2014). Well played: The origins and future of playfulness. *American Journal of Play*, 6(2), 234–266.

Gregory, E. (2008). *Learning to read in a new language: Making sense of words and worlds*. Sage.

Hännikäinen, M., & Munter, H. (2018). Toddlers' play in early childhood education settings. In P. K. Smith & J. L. Roopnarine (Eds.), *Cambridge handbook of play: Developmental and disciplinary perspectives* (pp. 491–510). Cambridge University Press. doi:10.1017/9781108131384.027.

Heath, S. B. (1983). *Ways with words: Language, life and work in communities and classrooms*. Cambridge University Press.

Hedegaard, M. (2020). Children's exploration as a key in children's play and learning activity in social and cultural formation. In M. Hedegaard & E. E. Odegaard (Eds), *Children's exploration and cultural formation* (pp. 11–28). Springer.

Jones, E., & Reynolds, G. (2015). *The play's the thing: Teachers' roles in children's play.* Teachers College Press.

Kavanaugh, R. D. (2011). Origins and consequences of social pretend play. In P. Nathan & A. D. Pellegrini (Eds.), *The Oxford handbook of the development of play* (pp. 296–307). Oxford University Press.

Kind, S. (2014). Material encounters. *International Journal of Child, Youth and Family Studies*, 5(4.2), 865–877.

King, H. (2007). *The language barrier: A handbook for parents & teachers.* Trafford.

Leiberman, P. (2010). From grunting to gabbing: Why humans can talk. Retrieved from www.npr.org/templates/story/story.php?storyId=129083762\

Li, L., Ridgway, A., & Quiñones, G. (2021). Moral imagination: Creating affective values through toddlers' joint play. *Learning, Culture and Social Interaction*, 30, 100435.

Maguire-Fong, M. J. (2014). *Teaching and learning with infants and toddlers: Where meaning-making begins.* Teachers College Press.

Majorano, M., Corsano, P., & Triffoni, G. (2015). Educators' intervention, communication and peers' conflict in nurseries. *Child Care in Practice*, 21(2), 98–113.

Mardell, B., Wilson, D., Ryan, J., Ertel, K., Krechevsky, M., & Baker, M. (2016). *Towards a pedagogy of play, and Project Zero working paper. The pedagogy of play research team.* Project Zero, Harvard University.

Meins, E., Fernyhough, C., Arnott, B., Leekam, S. R., & de Rosnay, M. (2013). Mind-mindedness and theory of mind: Mediating roles of language and perspectival symbolic play. *Child Development*, 84(5), 1777–1790.

Ninio, A., & Bruner, J. (1978). The achievement and antecedents of labelling. *Journal of Child Language*, 5(1), 1–15.

Nsamenang, A. B. (2005). Educational development and knowledge flow: Local and global forces in human development in Africa. *Higher Education Policy*, 18, 275–288.

Odegaard, E. E., & Hedegaard, M. (2020). Introduction to children's exploration and cultural formation. In M. Hedegaard & E. E. Odegaard (Eds.), *Children's exploration and cultural formation* (pp. 1–10). Springer.

Pellegrini, A. D. (2009). *The role of play in human development.* Oxford University Press.

Perry, T., & Delpit, L. (Eds.). (1998). *The real Ebonics debate: Power, language, and the education of African-American children.* Beacon Press.

Quiñones, G., Li, L., & Ridgway, A. (2021). *Affective early childhood pedagogy for infant-toddlers.* Springer.

Rogoff, B., Dahl, A., & Callanan, M. (2018). The importance of understanding children's lived experience. *Developmental Review*, 50, 5–15.

Smitherman, G. (2006). African American language: So good it's bad. In G. Smitherman (Ed.), *Word from the mother: Language as African Americans* (pp. 1–19). Routledge.

Snow, C. E. (1977). The development of conversation between mothers and babies. *Journal of Child Language*, 4(1), 1–22.

Souto-Manning, M. (2010). Challenging ethnocentric literacy practices: [Re] positioning home literacies in a head start classroom. *Research in the Teaching of English*, 45(2), 150–178.

Sutton-Smith, B. (1981). The social psychology and anthropology of play and games. In G. R. F. Lüschen, G. H. Sage, & L. Sfeir (Eds.), *Handbook of social science of sport* (pp. 452–478). Stipes Publishing Company.

Tannock, M. (2011). Observing young children's rough-and-tumble play. *Australasian Journal of Early Childhood*, 36(2), 13–20.

Tsao, Y. L. (2008). Using guided play to enhance children's conversation, creativity and competence in literacy. *Education*, 128(3), 515–520.

Vygotsky, L. S., & Cole, M. (1978). *Mind in society: Development of higher psychological processes.* Harvard University Press.

2 Organizational and Leadership Strategies for Promoting Language, Play, and Interaction

Nodelyn Abayan

Opening Reflections

1   What is the role of language, play, and interaction within your overall philosophy of infant and toddler care and education?
2   What kinds of coaching and modeling best support your strategies for linking language, play, and social interaction for infants and toddlers?

Introduction

I received my bachelor's degree in High School Education and a minor in Values Education in Manila, Philippines. I always knew that I wanted to be a teacher, and upon graduation I taught high school students for a year and elementary school students for a few years in the Philippines. Then, I changed course and found myself landing at Don Muang Airport in Bangkok, Thailand, ready to venture out to teach preschoolers. This is where my new journey into the world of early childhood education began. I taught at the International Montessori Preschool in Bangkok with 2- and 3-year-old children from different cultures. They taught me how to speak their languages, I easily learned Thai, and the children eventually learned Tagalog words from me in a mutual exchange of learning. I fell in love with the children and became curious about young children's language development skills and how they acquire it. Eventually, I settled in San Francisco, California where I first worked as an infant lead teacher at a university-based laboratory school before taking on my current role as the Infant Toddler Program Coordinator at the Early Childhood Education Center at San Francisco State University.

In this chapter, I describe our center's approach to infant and toddler care, and highlight key goals and strategies for linking language, play, and social interaction for young children. I also describe my roles as an administrator in supporting the teachers and teaching assistants at our center in strengthening how we integrate language, play, and interaction as the foundation for our curriculum and relationship-building.

Program for Infant/Toddler Care

The Program for Infant/Toddler Care (PITC) (Mangione et al., 2021) has been the most influential approach for my teaching and administration in infant and toddler programs. This approach emphasizes responsive, respectful care in relationships and intentional positive language to support children's holistic learning and development. Our center also integrates a Reggio-inspired play-based, emergent curriculum, in which infant and toddlers

DOI: 10.4324/9781003227816-4

are encouraged to use all their senses in their exploration, learning, and interactions. The Reggio approach "thinks of a school for young children as an integral living organism, as a place of shared lives and relationships among many adults and many children" (Gandini, 2012, p. 41). I continually work with the infant-toddler teachers to tighten the connections between the main elements of our curricular and language education (Figure 2.1)

Continuity of Care

Our center provides a high-quality staff-to-child ratio that we believe is the key determinant of quality caregiving and adheres to NAEYC accreditation standards (www.naeyc.org/our-work/families/10-naeyc-program-standards) and exceeds CA state licensing regulations (www.cdss.ca.gov/inforesources/child-care-licensing). The group size and/or ratios allow for the time and the staff needed to work individually with children as well support their social and language development.

We are one of the unique centers in the San Francisco Bay Area that integrates the fundamental philosophies and elements of PITC—Primary Care, Small Groups, Individualized Care, Culturally Responsive Care, Continuity of Care, and Inclusive Care (Mangione et al., 2021). Although Continuity of Care is the most challenging element to implement with consistency due to high staff turnover in our field, this remains the foundational element of our center's philosophy and care model. The continuity of care approach emphasizes the program-wide practice of assigning a primary caregiver or head teacher to each infant/toddler at the time of enrollment and continuing this relationship until the child is at least three years old. At our center, the head teacher begins in the infant classroom, follows the same group of children the next year into the toddler classroom and a new environment and then off to the transition

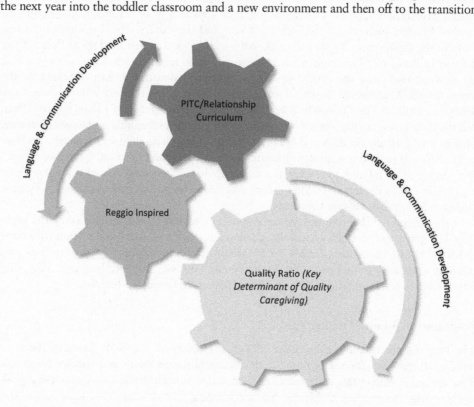

Figure 2.1 Key elements of our infant-toddler program and language education

or the 2's classroom. The classrooms are uniquely designed as a pod system in which both the infant and the toddler classrooms share the same pod. This kind of setting and environment helps promote language and communication between staff and the children (Figure 2.2).

As the head teachers and the children grow and learn together, the teachers' social, cognitive, and language goals and strategies for their group of children become increasingly sophisticated and complex.

In the preschool program, this same group of children stays together but joins new preschool teachers as the infant toddler teachers finish their loop when the children turn three, and then return to starting again with a new group of infants and young toddlers. As a university-based program, our teacher assistants are BA students taking coursework in Child Development and other disciplines. We design our staffing so that our teacher assistants usually stay with the same group of children for two years, though this can vary, to continue and strengthen the positive social attachments.

The promotion of healthy relationships for young children with peers and adults provides a long-term foundation of safety and trust to explore their worlds and learn from new experiences (Ahnert et al., 2006; Howes & Spieker, 2008). In our program, children feel supported and safe because they have consistent teachers for the first 3 years of their lives, which results in higher levels of social skills and self-help skills (Ruprecht et al., 2016). The children know that they have familiar and trusted adults who know them well and believe in what they can do. The teachers become acquainted with each child's temperament and personalities and can more effectively support each child's needs and growth as they get older. They also can follow the developmental progress and milestones

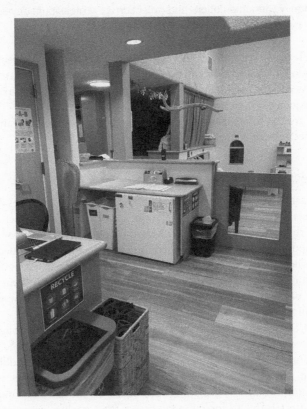

Figure 2.2 Our pod system

for language, play, and interaction for each child over their three years together. Of course, the children continually surprise us every day with the ways they think, interact, talk, and react. Over time, the teacher-child relationship becomes more natural, automatic, and interactive.

Supporting Language, Play, and Interaction—My Administrative Roles

In my current role as Infant and Toddler Program Coordinator, I lead our center's efforts to integrate language, play, and interaction for the infants and toddlers by:

1 In-classroom coaching and modeling for teachers and teacher assistants on how to effectively communicate with children in developmentally appropriate and culturally responsive ways.
2 Conducting a once-a-semester CLASS assessment in each classroom consisting of a 1–2-hour observation of teachers' communication and language with children.
3 Providing ongoing professional development focusing on inquiry, documentation, and reflection focused on children's language, play, and interaction.

Key Leadership Roles

- In-classroom modeling and coaching.
- In-classroom observations and assessments.
- Use of inquiry, documentation, and reflection as professional development.

In doing so, I work with the teachers to hone our overall philosophy of language learning as founded upon social interaction and dialogic learning. Our program highlights four key elements for our teaching, assessments, and inquiry work: (1) receptive language; (2) expressive language; (3) communication skills and knowledge; and (4) interest in print. These elements are the foundation for my coaching and modeling of language, play, and interaction connections in the classrooms.

Coaching and Modeling

On a regular basis I work with teachers both indoors and outdoors to support play, language, and social interaction for the children. I make sure that I spend quality time in each classroom that I supervise, and am aware of the potential impact of every single minute that I model for teachers how to communicate and interact effectively with children. I have learned that it takes time and practice for early childhood practitioners to create meaningful communication and language magic, and so as an administrator I create a flexible professional teaching and learning environment to support both novice and more veteran teachers.

I also support teachers by providing training and development through my classroom observations using the Classroom Assessment Scoring System (CLASS) assessment tool developed by Pianta, La Paro, and Hamre (2009) in both infant and toddler versions. The CLASS approach provides me with foundational ideas and strategies to articulate our language, play, and interaction goals and techniques on the floor for our teaching team. For example, I use CLASS to look for key ways that teachers integrate nonverbal and verbal communication:

- Linking teachers' actions with specific oral language (e.g., "I am going to stand to prepare the diaper table for you" or "I am going to the sink to wash my hands").
- Narrating children's actions with language (e.g., "Qixia, you picked up that rattle and shook it" or "Diana, you are crawling towards the ball").
- Repeating and extending children's communication attempts and language (e.g., A young toddler attempts to say, "Ball" and the teacher extends their language by saying "Yes, the blue ball!").

When I meet with teachers to share my observations, the tool helps us reflect on ways that teachers can deepen the quality of interactions and language use with children. When we work with children with disabilities, we use the same tool as for the rest of the children. This tool also provides a consistent language education foundation that I can share with new teachers and teaching assistants as they enter our infant and toddler program. I also use CLASS to help me coordinate and collaborate with the other administrators in the center to create policy to articulate and plan our infants and toddler language education.

In my own interactions with children in the classrooms, I intentionally model this integration of nonverbal and verbal language and communication for the teachers through both planned and spontaneous support both indoors and outside. For example, I sit with four children (ages 6–9 months) on the floor and use exaggerated facial expressions to engage with them (Figure 2.3).

I intentionally interact with children to promote the social aspects of communication through engaging in turn-taking behavior in proto conversations. In these conversations,

Figure 2.3 I interact with four infants on the floor by using exaggerated facial expressions

the adult speaks to the preverbal infant, and the infant responds by making eye contact, cooing, smiling, gesturing. These "conversation-like" interactions go back and forth between the adult and the infant for several turns, helping infants to bond with adults and promote a sense of joy and contentment in their interactions (California Department of Education, 2009, p. 43).

Overall, in my coaching and mentoring in the classrooms, I rely on several key language development strategies (Program for Intant/Toddler Care, WestEd, www.wested.org/project/program-for-infant-toddler-care) (Table 2.1).

In my coaching and modeling in classrooms, I adapt these strategies to individual children depending on their age and temperament and language talents and interests, as well as to the specific professional goals individual teachers have for supporting children's language development. I also continually model and interact with infants and toddler on the floor to deepen my own awareness and skill in understanding and meeting their language, play, and interactional needs.

Assessments

Our center is partially funded by First 5 San Francisco, part of the San Francisco Office of Early Care and Education, and they conduct a Quality Rating and Improvement System (QRIS) (Isner et al., 2011). QRIS uses the Early Childhood Environmental Rating Scale/Infant Toddler Environmental Rating Scale (ECERS/ITERS) and the aforementioned CLASS tool for Infants and Toddlers. The use of ECERS and ITERS helps us evaluate the classroom environments for language learning, and CLASS helps us focus on the overall quality of social and language interactions.

Early Childhood Environmental Rating Scale/ Infant Toddler Environmental Rating Scale (ECERS/ITERS)

ECERS and ITERS are classroom assessment tools designed to measure the quality of group programs for infants and toddlers (ITERS for children ages 0–3 years old) and (ECERS for children ages 3–5 years). A certified assessor collects data through classroom observations and a staff interview. The first six subscales are referred to as child-related, and the items in the last subscale are referred to as parent-/staff-related. Each item is ranked from 1 to 7. A ranking of 1 describes care that does not meet custodial care needs while a ranking of 7 indicates excellent, high-quality personalized care. These assessment tools can be utilized as a form of self-assessment for teachers to reflect on the quality of language and environments in their classrooms, and to determine those elements that may need additional attention. I also use these assessments to create action plans for strengthening our language, play, and interactional approaches. For instance, I have used the "Interaction subscale" to determine topics to consider in developing training sessions for teachers and teacher assistants on specific aspects of children's language development.

Specific, Measurable, Achievable, Realistic and anchored within a Time Frame (SMART) Goals

I also adapted certain SMART (Specific, Measurable, Achievable, Realistic and anchored within Time Frame) (Conzemius & O'Neill, 2009) goals for the purpose of helping teachers create their goals specific to their professional growth. For example, during my classroom observation of the head teachers, I ask them to reflect on "how

Table 2.1 Language strategies to model with children and teachers

Strategy	Definition	Example
Be responsive when children initiate communication	As teachers, we are always aware of the sights and sounds of the children and environment. We learn how to recognize the various sounds that infants make so we can respond appropriately.	"I can see that you are looking at the wind-chimes, Elias, because you are wondering about the source of the sound."
Engage in non-verbal communication	Use of facial expressions in the back-and-forth exchanges with the infants and toddlers for varied in-the-moment reasons.	Teacher Helen smiled back at Athena when Athena giggled. Teacher Emily puts up her palm up to say, "STOP!" when Emilio tries to push another child.
Use self-talk and parallel talk	The narration of actions and feeling when playing, interacting, and interacting with infants and toddlers.	When teacher Helen needs to stand up to get something she says, "I am going to stand up to make your bottle" and engages in parallel talk when she describes what the child is doing while she is making the milk, "Oh, Leandra you are going up the loft. You're holding on to the railing, that is being safe."
Help children expand language	Co-construction with infants and toddlers through engaging in interactions of mutual interest.	Zev (age 2) and I sat in the kitchen/dramatic play area. We were naming the various plastic fruits and talking about how we can put some fruits in the pretend mix cake we are baking. I said, "I love mangos in my cake!" Zev said, "My favorite are blueberries! I love making blueberry cake!" I asked Zev, "Where do you think we can buy blueberry cake, Zev?" He stopped and thought for a moment and responded with so much enthusiasm, "The Blueberry Store!"

Engage infants and toddlers with books and stories	The careful creation of inviting areas and materials for book exploration and storytelling.	We have baskets of books in all the learning areas. For example, in the kitchen/dramatic area during a project on ice cream making, the teachers put together a basket full of books about ice cream. Infants and young toddlers can easily reach these books for playful book interactions and exploration.
		    For older toddlers, book engagement might involve verbal conversation as when 2-year-old Zev and I talked about a book:
		    Nodelyn: (opening a book and pointing to a picture of Corduroy, the brown bear) What kind of animal is Corduroy?
		    Zev: A bear!
		    Nodelyn: How do you know that this animal is a bear?
		    Zev: Because it's brown!

Be playful with language	The use of nonverbal and verbal language in playful ways that supports loving, enjoyable, and satisfying play and interaction.	Helen usually sings songs with the children by playing with the sounds of their names. e. g. "Willoughby wallaby wee, an elephant sat on me, Willoughby wallaby woo, an elephant sat on you, Willoughby wallaby wusten, an elephant sat on Justin, Willoughby wallaby wanya, an elephant sat on Tanya!"

many times did you repeat and extend children's communication attempts in a specific conversation?" I encourage them to increase the number of efforts for repetition and extension in conversations to three times, and we brainstorm new ways to work toward this goal.

Professional Growth, Inquiry, and Reflection

I place particular importance on the professional growth process of teacher inquiry, documentation, and reflection. For instance, the infant toddler team recently collaborated in a year-long nature inquiry group. I wanted our team to deepen our observational skills, and appreciate the children's learning, curiosity and discovery in nature and the outdoors. At our monthly inquiry group meetings, teachers shared their ongoing documentation of children's language, play, and social interaction within the context of making discoveries in nature. The team shared photographs, brief video clips, observational notes, and postings to our BAND app platform for our families. The nature inquiry group also encouraged our teaching team to spend more time outdoors with the infants and toddlers, as both the teachers and the children discovered new possibilities for language, play, and interaction outside. For example, teacher Helen reflected on the children's fascination with a bumblebee:

> Children were all looking at the bumble bee and saying, "Don't touch it" to each other while I described the various features of the bee and what bees do. I noticed while I was explaining this, the children were so focused on the dead bee. Leandra even went down on the ground to have a closer look. Other children on the other hand, noticed that there are other bees around.

This brief experience inspired Helen and her colleagues to expand their discoveries and research the life cycle of bees with the children.

Since we are also a Reggio-inspired program, we continually focus on adapting and changing our classroom environments to support children's language, play, and interactions. The process of teacher reflection supports our constant reflection on tinkering with our environments to best suit the children's developmental needs, facilitate quality language and social interactions with the children, promote a collaborative classroom teaching team, and model for parents how environments can serve children's language, play, and interactional needs and talents.

> An environment is a living, changing system. More than the physical space, it includes the way time is structured and the roles we are expected to play. It conditions how we feel, think, and behave; it dramatically affects the quality of our lives. The environment either works for us or against us as we conduct our lives.
>
> (Greenman, 1988, p. 5)

Since our center follows the university's academic calendar, we utilize the times we are closed as opportunities to reflect on and change the environment. Teachers carefully consider these changes as a team and often consult with me for recommendations and suggestions. Simultaneously, they are also meeting with the new families through a process we call "center visits." These visits help orient families to how we provide a meaningful and engaging environment to promote language, play, and interaction. In conversation with families, the teachers become more knowledgeable about the children and use this newfound information to adapt the environment.

Provocations—Observing and Documenting Children's Language, Play, and Interaction

A critical element in this process involves the use the Reggio Emilia idea of provocations, which are open-ended activities that stimulate children's minds, their imagination, and innate curiosity. Teacher inquiry, documentation, and reflection play key roles in discovering new provocations that are meaningful both to teachers and to the children. As we engage with the provocations, we also observe and document how and why children explore materials, hone their problem-solving skills through nonverbal and verbal communication, and observe with each other (Figures 2.4 and 2.5).

When we share our inquiry and documentation with families via the BAND app, we often highlight the children's engagement with these provocations. We want to emphasize how we create meaningful interactions that promote a high level of critical thinking and language use. For example, the teachers posted a brief snippet of documentation on the BAND app focused on how two-year-olds Zev and Dariya played together with trains (Figure 2.6):

Figure 2.4 Children observe and compare the growth rates of plants

Figure 2.5 Children observe and match color bean bags and rings

Figure 2.6 Zev and Alaya playing with the train tracks

The morning started out with Zev and Dariya working on building with trains and tracks together. Zev told Dariya. "I am making the track for Daly, Daly BART Station. You can work on the Embarcadero Station." After building their tracks, they connected trains together. Zev asked Dariya where she wanted to go and Dariya said, "We need to get on the bus to go home."

In their language-based and playful interactions, Zev referenced the accurate names of the BART stations, and Dariya worked with Zev to connect the trains and remind Zev that they needed to take the bus "to go home." This brief documented scene shows families how toddlers can create and enact their own developmentally appropriate and child responsive playful interactions using nonverbal and verbal communication.

Closing

The principle of continuity of care, one of the four PITC elements, is instrumental in supporting the language learning and development of infants and toddlers. Continuity of care provides a secure emotional base through the long-term promotion of healthy relationships with peers and adults and provides a foundation of safety to explore their world and play with objects and each other. As an administrator, I work toward deepening our language-rich environments and promoting professional development for teachers through coaching, modeling, and the process of inquiry, documentation, and reflection. It is a deeply rewarding experience for me to continually refine our connections between language, play, and interaction within our continuity of care model and Reggio-inspired curriculum.

Closing Reflections

1   What are the benefits of Nodelyn's infant-toddler program's approach to relationship-based care for linking children's language, play, and interaction?
2   What do you find effective about Nodelyn's coaching and mentoring strategies, and her program's use of teacher inquiry, documentation, and reflection?

References

Ahnert, L., Pinquart, M., & Lamb, M. E. (2006). Security of children's relationships with non-parental care providers: A meta-analysis. *Child Development*, 77(3), 664–679.

California Department of Education. (2009). California infant/toddler learning & development foundations. Retrieved from www.cde.ca.gov/sp/cd/re/documents/itfoundations2009.pdf.

Conzemius, A., & O'Neill, J. (2009). *The power of SMART goals: Using goals to improve student learning*. Solution Tree Press.

Gandini, L. (2012). History, ideas, and basic principles: An interview with Loris Malaguzzi. In C. P. Edwards, L. Gandini, L., & G. E. Forman (Eds.), *The hundred languages of children: The Reggio Emilia experience in transformation* (pp. 27–71). Ablex.

Greenman, J. T. (1988). *Caring spaces, learning spaces: Children's environments that work*. Exchange Press.

Howes, C., & Spieker, S. (2008). Attachment relationships in the context of multiple caregivers. In J. Cassidy & P. R. Shaver (Eds.), *Handbook of attachment: Theory, research, and clinical applications* (pp. 317–332). The Guilford Press.

Isner, T., Tout, K., Zaslow, M., Soli, M., Quinn, K., Rothenberg, L., & Burkhauser, M. (2011). *Coaching in early care and education programs and Quality Rating and Improvement Systems (QRIS): Identifying promising features*. Child Trends.

Mangione, P., Lally, J.R., Harkins, D.M, Morabito, A.O., with Paxton, A.R. (2021). *The PITC curriculum*. WestED.

Pianta, R. C., La Paro, K. M., & Hamre, B. K. (2009). *Classroom Assessment Scoring System: Infant Version*. Unpublished instrument.

Ruprecht, K., Elicker, J., & Choi, J. Y. (2016). Continuity of care, caregiver–child interactions, and toddler social competence and problem behaviors. *Early Education and Development*, 27(2), 221–239.

3 Establishing Indoor and Outdoor Play Environments for Language Growth

Emily Bugos

Opening Reflections

1 Can you think of a time when you communicated with an infant or toddler who understood you, but had not yet developed the verbal skills to respond? How did you know that they understood you?
2 What would you like to learn about designing and implementing indoor and outdoor learning environments to support young children's play, interaction, and language?

Introduction

Language is an essential element to communicate, make sense of the world, interact and build relationships, and seek comfort, enjoyment, and exploration (Davidson, 1998; Meier, 2004; Murphy, 2016; Yogman et al., 2018). Children play *with* language, use language *to* play, learn *how* to play through the use of language, and use language to *enhance* their play. I plan and assess for connections between play and language as I observe children's development over three years based upon my center's continuity of care approach, which my colleague Nodelyn Abayan described in the previous chapter. I also rely on the process of narrative inquiry and documentation (Edwards & Rinaldi, 2009; Sisk-Hilton & Meier, 2017) for observing, documenting, and reflecting on my teaching. In this chapter, I highlight how and why I connect the environment and materials, social interactions, and classroom routines to support child-led play, oral language, and nonverbal communication. The chapter follows my last three-year continuity of care journey with the same group of children.

Year 1—Routines as Language Curriculum

Starting as an infant teacher, I had to think differently about what, where, and how to place materials. My group of infants were between 4 and 10 months; none of the children was walking yet, and while some could sit up on their own, most were non-mobile and not yet using spoken language. As soon as the semester started, I felt stressed by their crying and physical attempts to make their needs known by reaching for me and clinging to my body. I wondered, how could I implement a language curriculum with nonverbal infants? How could I focus on *any* sort of curriculum when my arms were full of children in need of comfort and love and reassurance? Nodelyn spent hours in my classroom each day, holding babies, singing to them, and showing me that my language curriculum was *already* happening.

DOI: 10.4324/9781003227816-5

So routines became my curriculum. Within each of our routines—diaper changes, nap times, meals, free play, and transitions between school and home—I reflected on how these moments connected language to our environment and our social relationships. Consistent, responsive routines build a sense of security as infants get to know new people and a new space, and this fostering of safety and belonging is founded upon how we use language and communicate with infants. As an infant cries to communicate hunger, I say, "I hear you are so hungry. I am putting your bottle in the warmer. It will be ready soon. I can sit with you while we wait." When I change a baby's diaper, I talk to them about the steps involved and encourage them to hold and touch the diaper cream. I sing, pause, and give them time to respond. When I feed children, we sit face to face so we can see each other's expressions as I speak. I talk to them about the feeling of the water when they wash their hands. I imitate their words and sounds as they talk and play. I keep these interactional routines consistent and repeat the same words to build familiarity as Hirsh-Pasek and Golinkoff (2012) recommend, "opportunities to hear and respond to language support children's growing vocabulary and grammar" (p. 88).

Interactions—Promoting Language through Building Trust

In addition to engaging with my colleagues and me during routine caregiving moments such as feeding, diapering, and napping, infants play and freely explore indoor and outdoor spaces, including activities such as painting, sensory, and music. I use a calm approach in my interactions with infants to create a sense of security and trust that sets the foundation for language learning. For example, I use eye contact and a gentle tone of voice during meals and bottle feedings and speak with the babies as I feed them (Figure 3.1).

Figure 3.1 Eye contact during bottle feeding

They smile at my voice, with milk dribbling out of their mouths, or wrap their chubby hands around my finger and gurgle. I also consider my body position, and the position of the children, and how these face-to-face interactions support language development and communication. The children watch my mouth as I form words, gauge my facial expressions and reactions, notice my body language in relation to my words and tone, and connect what I am holding or pointing at with my spoken words. During these face-to-face interactions, I am either holding the infants, sitting across from them at a table, or lying face to face. During free play, I position non-mobile infants together with materials to encourage peer interaction. I then observe to see how they imitate each other's language; as one baby babbles or coos, the other repeats the same sound; when one shrieks, so does the other; when one cries, often the other does as well.

Physical Environment and Materials—Setting the Scene for Relationships and Routines

I arrange my classroom through a lens of social relationships and language development as I consider the placement of furniture and materials and determine the type of items and toys available. Everything in the physical environment feels new to an infant. Each object is an opportunity for social and language growth. The items in the physical environment provide avenues for us to introduce language. In setting up an infant classroom or outdoor space, I think about where and how to place materials to invite exploration and movement—crawling, rolling, bending, pulling up, climbing, reaching, gripping, and walking. As children move throughout the space, I talk to them about what their bodies are doing and what they are discovering. I intentionally include open-ended materials as these offer unlimited possibilities for creativity, expression, critical thinking, and problem-solving, and encourage and strengthen children's language. Indoors, we offer wooden rings, empty containers, scarves, or cardboard boxes, and outdoors we arrange blocks, fabrics, and milk crates.

I rotate materials as infants develop rather than on a set schedule. As they become mobile and begin crawling, walking, or pulling up, I might flip a riser for them to climb in and out. As they learn to grip, I take away smaller gripping toys and add in different sizes, weights, and textures. As they stop mouthing books, I remove the soft fabric books and add touch-and-feel books. I also find it best to have cozy, cushioned play spaces outdoors, especially for younger infants who are not yet sitting up. This can include blankets or pillows, as well as books, musical instruments, textured toys, and gripping rings. I position these cozy spaces so that infants can freely explore the natural elements outdoors—under a tree to watch the leaves move in the wind or near flowers or plants for touching and smelling. When the environment offers invitations to explore freely, this creates opportunities for us to use self-talk and narration to describe the goings-on and for infants to hear and make associations to words, sounds, people, and routines. Striking a balance between repetition and novelty—consistent materials alongside new materials—allows infants to hear us say both familiar and unfamiliar vocabulary and expand their receptive and expressive vocabulary (Figure 3.2).

To broaden children's receptive vocabulary, I use specific and technical vocabulary along with descriptive language as Camille Dungy advised, when observing and interacting with her infant daughter, "If she looks toward an orange flower, call it what it is, *California poppy*. Bring her body closer to the flower and linger awhile so she can come to know it in her own way" (Dungy, 2020, pp. 61–62). Dungy also highlights the value of sitting back and allowing play and discovery to unfold organically while offering words to support infants' learning—"Don't work too hard to choreograph the child's encounter. Give it time. What will she do? How will she feel? How will you talk to her to help her understand what she's feeling?" (p. 62).

Figure 3.2 Theo exploring soap suds as I describe them

For example, outside in the garden with 16-month-old Ronan, I described the "tiny red petals" as he stared intently at the bunches of flowers and gently touched them (Figure 3.3).

After watching Ronan stare at the flowers for several moments, I reached out and gently touched the flowers with my fingertip. Ronan looked at me, then back at the flowers, as he reached out to touch them with his own fingertip. I said, "It feels velvety. Soft. What do you think?" and then left space for his own thoughts and response as he stated, "Fower." This moment required no choreography or forethought, and our verbal and physical interaction arose organically, and as I took Ronan's lead through my use of gesture, touch, and oral language, I supported Ronan's interest in the flowers.

Year 2—The Bees Who Helped Us Say Goodbye

As the children reached their first birthdays, we moved up as a group to the toddler classroom. During our first week in the toddler room, a small group of us sat outside on the grass and observed a nearby bee. The children kept their fascinated gazes on the bee as it flew around their bodies. I narrated the bee's movements and repeated words and sounds as the children watched and listened.

EMILY: The bee is flying.
CHILDREN: [following bee with their gaze]
EMILY: I can hear the bee making a bzzzz sound.
DIANA: Bzzzzz. Bee!
EMILY: Yes, it's saying "bzzzzz" while it flies.

Figure 3.3 Ronan examining flowers as I describe the sight, smell, and texture

As the bee flew away, Diana raised her arms in a shrug, as if to ask, "Where did it go?" I attempted to help her verbalize her communication.

EMILY: [tapping my chin] Hmmm ... where did it go?
HAYLEY: [looking at me and tapping her chin]
DIANA: [tapping her chin] Hmmm ... where go?

Since I wanted to keep the children from being fearful of the bee, I voiced the bee's actions and kept a calm body and voice.

During this same week, some of the children had difficulty separating from their families during drop-off and cried as their parents attempted to leave. I used this prior small moment with the bee to help the children transition each morning. Each morning at drop-off, I empathized with the crying children, matching my tone, words, and facial expressions to their feelings. As they began to calm, I offered, "I wonder if you'd like to go look for the bees. That made you very happy the other day." By focusing on and exploring our new area of interest, I consoled the children and supported their growing receptive and expressive vocabulary.

Interactions

The repetition and consistency of our daily bee search exposed the children to the same words, allowing them to hear, build, and practice their expressive language—"children learn the words that they hear the most" (Hirsh-Pasek & Golinkoff, 2012, p. 88). Our daily interactions also provided opportunities for the children to relate words to objects, and to "learn words for things and events that interest them" (pp. 88–89). At first, every bug we found was a "bee." Over time, the children learned that bees have wings and fuzzy black and yellow bodies and were often found near our cherry blossom tree. I started each bee search by tapping my chin and repeating, "Hmmmm … where did they go?" The children quickly picked up on the concept of words as attached to gestures and expressions. Soon, they began to frown, tap their chins, and shrug as they wondered aloud, "Where go?" and "Bee?"

Expanding the Children's Interest in Bees—Exploring the Outdoors

As our interest in bees continued, I thought about ways to expand the children's language learning through more hands-on experiences with the natural world. Our outdoor space housed a small garden and I wondered aloud if the bees might be enjoying our mint plant. Diana lifted up a rock, under which was a large worm. The other children leaned in, eyes widening. Diana's discovery helped me realize that while we could not explore live bees with all of our senses, we could certainly expand our explorations and language learning with many other outdoor natural objects. Since the children mostly used three-word sentences and were not making many verbal predictions, I supported their physical discoveries to promote critical thinking and to spark curiosity. I placed shovels in the garden for digging, gathered books about worms and insects, and brought soil and worms into the classroom on shallow trays and observed through magnifying glasses (Figures 3.4 and 3.5).

Figure 3.4 Exploring worms indoors and outdoors provides opportunities for language

Figure 3.5 Exploring worms indoors and outdoors and opportunities for language expansion and conversation as children explore colors, textures, sights, and sounds

We learned that worms help us compost food and we placed banana peels in the garden. Our new explorations of nature both inside and outside the classroom promoted new hands-on learning, which introduced new words for the children to learn. How do children really learn the meaning of the words "slippery" and "smooth" to describe a worm's body if they never get to feel it? Whether they were tasting mint, holding worms, or listening to bees buzzing around flowers, these magical garden moments allowed the children to explore their surroundings with all their senses, strengthening their physical connection to nature, elevating their moods, and sparking our collective language of wonder and curiosity.

Year 3—The Ice Cream Project—Building on Children's Emerging Interests Through Language

In my last year at the center, the children and I moved up to a transition classroom. Sophia, my co-teacher, and I observed the children playing "ice cream." They stood inside the outdoor playhouses while offering handfuls of tire chips out the window and shouted, "Ice cream!" This quickly became a favorite game that trickled over into the sandbox. Soon, ice cream creations filled buckets and measuring cups and were placed on the tree stumps that the children used for tables. Ice cream play became part of their daily play routine both indoors and outdoors.

Interactions—Introducing the Language of Wondering and Imagining

During ice cream play, Sophia and I used the "I wonder" phrase to provoke the children's thinking, and to invite "both children and teachers to make predictions and share ideas"

(Sisk-Hilton, 2020, p. 22). When they created ice cream scoops in the sandbox, we pondered aloud with the children, "I wonder what ingredients we might need?" and "I wonder how you are going to make that flavor?" The children shared their thoughts with responses such as, "I add sugar" or "Put it in the oven" or "You mix it." Through these play interactions and moments that encouraged imagination and critical thinking, we learned about the children's emerging ideas around how ice cream is made, including the ingredients (salt, sugar, milk), physical actions (shaking, mixing, stirring), and equipment (ice cream maker and whisk) needed. We continued to build on the children's language throughout our play and conversations. When a child requested, "Scoop please," we verbally expanded on their request by offering, "Here is your scoop of vanilla in a cone." We also incorporated more open-ended questions into our daily interactions, asking children to share their predictions and use their reasoning as they thought about our "how" and "why" and "what if" questions. Our intentional phrasing and use of open-ended questions encouraged the children to engage in conversation and storytelling, connect cognitive skills with language, and enhance their use and understanding of words in a socially-motivating pretend play context.

Physical Environment and Materials—Supporting Children's Emerging Interests and Language

The children's imaginations were vibrant—the sand was ice cream, the leaves were ice cream, the air was ice cream. To expand their language in these pretend play scenarios, we added a variety of materials to the indoor and outdoor spaces. We created an ice cream shop in the dramatic play space with a cash register, money, and popsicles created with the children's art. We added recyclable containers with pictures of ice cream to the sandbox. We made ice cream menus and posted pictures of ice cream treats from around the world. Families donated ice cream sets, complete with scoops of ice cream, cones, sprinkles, and fancy bowls. Typically, we strategically have more than one of each item available to the children. However, some of the more coveted donations, such as the ice cream sprinkles, did not have duplicates. Rather than removing these, we used them as a way to work through peer conflicts using our words. As we actively took on the role of participant by engaging in the children's play (Jones & Reynolds, 2015), we modeled phrases, turn-taking, and positive descriptive acknowledgment. The children also learned how to ask for a turn to communicate their wants and needs to listen and respond to others—they took ice cream orders over the "phone" and engaged in interactions over the cash register. Families also sent in photos of their children having ice cream at home and around the city, which we posted in the classroom to spark further conversation.

Routines—Building on Children's Knowledge through Language and Literacy

Our group time and free play routines allowed the children to dive into a pretend world of ice cream treats where they shared stories, worked through conflicts, imitated each other's words and movements, and interacted with materials. While many children chose to play together in their ice cream adventures, some chose to play alone and practiced their language skills by talking out loud to themselves without the need to process another's words or think about forming a response. The child-initiated pretend play of selling ice cream on the playground encouraged us to enhance the play environment and broaden the children's language and interactions as older toddlers around a shared play interest (Figure 3.6).

We also introduced new library books about ice cream trucks and factories, scoop shops and recipes, and stories about animals and people sharing ice cream together. We

Figure 3.6 Serving ice cream from the ice cream truck we created outside

labeled our ice cream items with pictures and words to further their exposure to written language and help them associate print with objects. We also made ice cream cookbooks and menus for the scoop shop and incorporated library books about ice cream into our classroom community routines for reading, singing, movement, conversations, and other activities. We also introduced and reinforced new vocabulary words as we learned about innovative flavors and toppings and read stories about *paletas* in Mexico and saffron ice cream in Iran. While we continued to provide consistency through our regular group time and play routines, we increased access to a wider range of interest-based materials in the indoor and outdoor environments, which enriched the children's interactions with us, each other, and the classroom materials.

Final Thoughts

This chapter describes how I plan indoor and outdoor language environments for the same children over our three years together, and create an evolving repertoire of caring interactional routines around play and active discovery-making (Table 3.1).

I also offer goals and strategies for building a language-rich environment based on trusting, foundational relationships established through consistency and responsiveness, as well as through adults' willingness to engage as active partners in play (Quiñones et al., 2021). Supporting the same group of children over three years allowed me to observe each child's language growth, and the use of stories and inquiry helped me document each child's language learning as well as that of the collective group. The process of inquiry, documentation, and reflection also helped me to plan for indoor and outdoor environments that supported each child's language as their social interaction and play developed from birth to age three.

Closing Reflections

1   What are the language, play, and social benefits of working with the same group infants and toddlers over the course of three years as Emily describes in this chapter?
2   In reflecting on the story of the bees, how does Emily use narration to deepen the children's interest and integrate language, play, and interaction?

Table 3.1 Indoor and outdoor strategies for language environments for children 0–3

Physical Environment and Materials	• Labels with visuals and words for all materials, toys, manipulatives, items, areas/centers of the room • Books easily accessible in indoor and outdoor play areas • Create accessible and interactive wall spaces that showcase photos, writing, posters, children's work hung at children's eye levels • Rotate materials based on children's interest, replacing unused toys/materials, and adding new toys/materials as needed
Routines	• Help children understand how their world is organized by keeping routines consistent • Strengthen children's vocabulary development by verbalizing steps of routines as they are happening • Support children's learning of social roles through participation in routines • Develop children's transitional skills by incorporating routine language ("In 2 minutes, we will ...") • Encourage children's language development by singing during routines
Interactions	• Repetition, self-talk, narration, and child-directed speech • Imitate sounds • Open-ended questions • Opportunities for conversation • Pause and allow children to respond verbally and nonverbally • Position your body intentionally to make and notice eye contact, gestures, and facial expressions • Use specific and descriptive language when naming things • Think aloud • Offer affirmations rather than prohibitions • Consider tone, body language/position, and nonverbal communication

References

Davidson, J. F. (1998). Language and play: Natural partners. In D. P. Fromberg & D. Bergen (Eds.), *Play from birth to twelve and beyond: Context, perspectives, and meanings* (pp. 175–183). Garland.

Dungy, C. T. (2020). Babies and nature: The act of noticing in infancy. In D. R. Meier & S. Sisk-Hilton (Eds.), *Nature education with young children: Integrating inquiry and practice* (2nd ed., pp. 53–65). Routledge.

Edwards, C. P. & Rinaldi, C. (2009). *The diary of Laura: Perspectives on a Reggio Emilia diary.* Redleaf Press.

Hirsh-Pasek, K., Golinkoff, R. M., & Eyer, D. (2004). *Einstein never used flash cards: How our children really learn–and why they need to play more and memorize less.* Rodale Books.

Hirsh-Pasek, K. & Golinkoff, R. M. (2012). How babies talk: Six principles of early language development. In S. L. Odom, E. P. Pungello, & N. Gardner-Neblett (Eds.), *Infants, toddlers, and families in poverty* (pp. 77–100). Guildford.

Jones, E., & Reynolds, G. (2015). *The play's the thing: Teachers' roles in children's play.* Teachers College Press.

Meier, D. (2004). *The young child's memory for words.* Teachers College Press.

Murphy, L. (2016). *Lisa Murphy on play: The foundation of children's learning.* Redleaf.

Quiñones, G., Li, L., & Ridgway, A. (2021). *Affective early childhood pedagogy for infant-toddlers.* Springer.

Sisk-Hilton, S. (2020). Science, nature, and inquiry-based learning in early childhood. In D. R. Meier & S. Sisk-Hilton (Eds.), *Nature education with young children: Integrating inquiry and practice* (2nd ed.) (pp. 11–30). Routledge.

Sisk-Hilton, S. & Meier, D. (2017). *Narrative inquiry in early childhood and elementary school: Learning to teach and teaching well*. Routledge.

Yogman, M., Garner, A., Hutchinson, J., Hirsh-Pasek, K., & Golinkoff, R. M. (2018). The power of play: A pediatric role in enhancing development in young children. *Pediatrics*, 142(3). https://pediatrics.aappublications.org/content/142/3/e20182058.

Part II

Language and Culture

4 Social and Cultural Contexts
Implications for Infant and Toddler Language Development

Iliana Alanís and Iheoma U. Iruka

Opening Reflections

1 What do you see as the role of socialization and culture in the language and literacy learning of infants and toddlers?
2 How does this view influence your philosophy of language and literacy education for young children and their families?

In this chapter, we examine research and theory on key intersections between cultural traditions and worldviews and the language learning of infants and toddlers. We emphasize the significance of enriching early learning experiences for children's long-term educational and life success, and view infants and toddlers as critical members of many interwoven communities in which even the youngest member participates. Consequently, we focus on the social and language-based interactions of infants and toddlers with key adults and other children both at home and in the community. We conclude with practices and policies that support an anti-bias and equitable education for young children's sociocultural and language growth.

The first three years of a child's life are crucial for overall development, particularly language development. This early development is a complex social and cognitive phenomenon shaped by the sociocultural contexts of children's lived experiences and relationships with others where children acquire language "within their society of language users" (Piper, 2003, p. 9). Children's socialization into a group's cultural practices is largely mediated through language, as it is through interaction with others that they learn the skills and concepts valued within their culture (Rogoff, 2003). In home and community settings, adults and older children use culturally empowered language experiences and activities to immerse infants and toddlers in local, contextualized language and literacy traditions often rooted in families' countries of origin preserved over generations. Given the inextricable link of language practices with educator's social and pedagogical beliefs and ideologies (Flores & Rosa, 2015), cultural beliefs, values, and practices of minoritized communities lay the foundation for children's language development.

Much of the research on children's early language experiences and development has focused on the White, middle-class, English-speaking population. The US Census, however, confirms the diversity of the country, showing the increase of more children of Color (53%) compared to White children (47%) (US Census, 2018). Children of Color include Latino, Black/African American, Asian American, American Indian/Alaska Native, Hawaiian/Other Pacific Islander, and multi-racial. Consequently, many children

DOI: 10.4324/9781003227816-7

are raised in multicultural and multilingual homes with unique developmental stories. As ECEs engage in developmentally appropriate and culturally responsive teaching, powerful language education is founded upon the multifaceted lives of children and their families (National Association for the Education of Young Children, 2019). This understanding leads to anti-racist and equitable language practices in educational settings (Allen et al., 2021), which create an inclusive lens for discussing the sociocultural roots and talents of children's linguistic development.

Theoretical Framework

In Bronfenbrenner's bio-ecological framework (Bronfenbrenner & Morris, 2007), development is dependent on nested systems that are proximal and distal. The microsystem is the closest to children and includes families and early care and education programs the mesosystem connects across systems such as those between families and educators, and the exosystem indirectly influences children's development such as their parents' work environment or neighborhoods. The most distal macrosystem includes the values and policies that indirectly impact children's development, such as whether children's needs are centered above adults. Bronfenbrenner's influential framework, though, neglects the sociocultural and political histories experienced by minoritized communities whose ways of being and language use are "othered."

In response to this lack of attention to culture in developmental science, García Coll and colleagues developed an integrated model for the study of developmental competencies of minority children (García Coll et al., 1996). This framework identifies how gender, race, ethnicity, and immigration status influence children's developmental and linguistic competencies and skills. This model highlights how minoritized communities face residential, economic, social, and psychological segregation because of oppressive and discriminatory policies and practices. These segregated environments are likely to result in the quality of home and out-of-home environments that children experience as adaptive responses to these exclusionary practices. Minoritized children exist in dual worlds where they develop skills that help them thrive within their culture and also the dominant culture. For instance, children may begin to engage in translanguaging practices that include code-switching where they use two languages to communicate and make meaning (García & Wei, 2014).

Key Idea

Translanguaging includes bilingual children's ability to:

1   use multiple language skills and varied resources to communicate and gain understanding;
2   use gestures such as pointing or facial expressions to communicate their feelings and needs; and
3   pay attention to language cues to determine what languages to use and with whom.

From an early age, then, children learn to engage in unique linguistic practices as part of their development and learning.

Language Development as a Continuum

Although language development is affected by many factors, including age, prior language experiences, and the home environment, all children are born with the capacity to learn multiple languages and different communication patterns (National Academies of Sciences, Engineering, and Medicine, 2017). For many infants and toddlers, their language development will include elements from two or more languages. Language development in bilingual or multilingual homes is a complex and dynamic process that leads to a great deal of variability (e.g. see Chapters 7–9 in this volume). Often young children interact for significant amounts of time with one individual who strongly influences their language environment. Grandparents, for example, may be the primary caregivers and important language models for the young child. As a result, we should consider the heterogeneity of children's linguistic environments and the complexity of children's linguistic repertoires. To appreciate young children's language development, we must acknowledge and respect the unique characteristics of every family's sophisticated language systems.

Language Development across Contexts

Children learn and play in the context of meaningful and productive activities within families and communities who are the primary sources for learning about their world (National Association for the Education of Young Children, 2020). A study of Latino bilingual 25-month-olds, for example, indicated that mothers and fathers were infants' conversational partners and accounted for 77% of the infants' conversations (Place & Hoff, 2016). This study determined that the input provided by native speakers was a predictor of language development and advanced the notion that language acquisition depends on the quantity and quality of children's language input.

Although we are often reminded that parents are children's first teachers, we frequently overlook other significant resources such as siblings, grandparents, and community members. Research illuminates the powerful language and literacy practices carried out by siblings and adults in intergenerational familial, home, and community settings (Tamis-LeMonda et al., 2019). These practices are often rooted in spiritual beliefs and values such as oral storytelling practices passed down from generation to generation, conversations embedded in home and community tasks, nonverbal and verbal modeling, and lessons taught by community elders.

Sociocultural Context of Language Development

Effective ECEs acknowledge the role that languages play in the home environment and families' lives as adults and siblings scaffold children's language through singing songs, sharing stories, engaging in book reading conversations, and talking during daily care routines (Farver et al., 2013). Families engage in numerous formal and informal language practices that provide the foundation for children's ways of knowing, thinking, and acting. Children's language development needs to be understood within the contexts of these sociocultural values and beliefs. Here we focus on the tradition of oral storytelling.

Storytelling

Children listen to and participate in storytelling within their families and communities, a process that supports children's socio-cultural development and enhances language development. How families share stories depends on families' cultural traditions but may include family history, folk tales, and life events (Gardner-Neblett et al., 2012). Story-telling in minoritized communities reflects a form of cultural wealth (Yosso, 2005) where families engage in pedagogies of the home (Delgado-Bernal, 2001).

Key Idea

Community cultural wealth (Yosso, 2005) involves the talents, strengths, and skills that children of Color bring to educational contexts. It also encompasses the knowledge, skills, and abilities used by minoritized communities to resist racism and other forms of oppression.

Oral storytelling is a critical way that families share generational and cultural knowledge and support children to become knowledge holders (Delgado-Bernal, 2001) who learn from the experiences of others (Tamis-LeMonda & Song, 2012). Through stories, families strengthen connections, teach values, and share cultural lessons. Storytelling creates opportunities to hear rich language, repetition, and rhyming, which develop expressive and receptive language skills. As a result, children who participate frequently in storytelling are more likely to have strong expressive and receptive language skills.

The Linguistic Influence of Siblings

Many children in the US live in intergenerational households, including multiple siblings, grandparents, and other relatives. The populations most likely to live with grand-parents are Native Hawaiians and other Pacific Islanders (9.9%), Latinos (7.1%), and children of Asian descent (5.6%) (US Census, 2016). Therefore, to understand children's language experiences, we must discover the multiple activities children engage in with family members and the family structures that provide rich language environments.

Young children are acculturated into various language forms and discourses through interactions and modeling from older siblings who are often responsible for caretaking and teaching young children in the home (Volk & de Acosta, 2004). Kibler et al. (2020) found that older siblings within immigrant families engaged in a variety of language practices during daily interactions while children played games or cared for pets. Cycyk and Hammer (2020) discovered that older children were consistent participants in many toddlers' activities and, often, the main individuals playing with toddlers. Toddlers' language comprehension improved due to the siblings' more complex and challenging language environment. Researchers also discovered that older siblings play a primary role in teaching communication skills and supporting early language and learning in English, perhaps as a result of siblings having more exposure to English at school (Malmeer & Assadi, 2013).

The Linguistic Influence of the Community

The multi-strand networks of family and community relationships mediate and contribute to children's language development. Guardado (2008) for example, found that groups of Latino families met at a community center weekly to maintain their children's connections to their cultural roots and practices and foster home language practices. These meetings facilitated both the maintenance of the home language and familial cultural traditions within their new setting.

Within Black communities, the church has a longstanding and important social and economic support and protective role (Thompson McMillon & Edwards, 2008). Black churches are an important institution for supporting families' access to basic resources like shelter, food, or emergency cash assistance and childcare. Historically, Black grandmothers have held the role of educators among family members and the wider community (Ruiz, 2008). Stephens, Carter-Francique, and McClain (2020) found that by infusing elements such as preaching, scripture reading, and the sharing of Biblical stories and faith-based teachings from the Black church, grandmothers contributed to children's learning and development including language practices, discourse patterns, and literacy traditions.

Families are experts in children's development and good observers of the languages that children hear and see in their homes and community settings. How do we tap into that knowledge, and increase opportunities for children to engage in meaningful language and play interactions? In the next section, we discuss developmentally, culturally, and linguistically appropriate practices for infant/toddler language development.

Equitable Practices that Support Language Development

Early childhood language environments predict meaningful differences in language and cognitive development (National Institute of Child Health and Human Development Early Child Care Research Network, 2000). Unfortunately, children and families often experience an uneven distribution of power that affects their relationships with educators and children's learning outcomes (Alanís et al., 2021). Given that early care and education settings for infants and toddlers are one of the fastest growing forms of child care (Cui & Natzke, 2021), educators must understand the sociocultural and political contexts of development including the interrelationship of language, culture, and learning to create culturally responsive and sustaining learning contexts (National Academies of Sciences, Engineering, and Medicine, 2017). For example, the daily integration of culturally relevant picture books and oral stories supports children's cultural knowledge, linguistic identity, and prior experiences (Castro & Franco, 2021).

Research indicates, however, that infant educators often lack a clear understanding of how to promote language for all children (Torr & Pham, 2016), and are susceptible to implicit biases regarding children's culture, race, or home language (Alanís et al., 2021). Nonetheless, a valuable part of infant/toddler language development is positive relationships with others who engage children as active participants in culturally responsive exchanges across different classroom activities (Castro & Franco, 2021). These also include oral activities that connect with children's cultural and linguistic experiences such as the riddles, rhymes, and songs that children hear at home and within their community (Alanís et al., 2019).

Infants and toddlers display agency through active roles in their language learning experiences and are effective communicators. From a very young age, children seek to interact with others (Trevarthen & Bjørkvold, 2016) and expect others to respond to their smile or vocalization (Markova & Legerstee, 2006). Individuals in the child's environment need to be attentive to the culturally nuanced ways that infants and toddlers communicate, which strengths a trusting child–adult relationship.

Effective educators impact children's learning and development by engaging in developmentally and linguistically appropriate strategies and recognizing each child's unique strengths (National Association for the Education of Young Children, 2020). These linguistic and strategic supports, which help children take risks with language and develop their agency as active participants in play and interactions, include extensions and recasting of children's language, recognizing communication attempts, and reciprocal conversations (Reilly et al., 2020).

Adults provide language support (scaffolding) through verbal expansions as they question children to expand on what they have said. When adults expand or recast children's communication attempts, they use new vocabulary and/or grammatical structures (syntax, morphology, semantics) that are just slightly above children's oral language level, thereby increasing their linguistic repertoire. This creates a natural, authentic opportunity for language learning. These language facilitating strategies are most effective when they are part of children's immediate experiences and culturally relevant topics. For example, when three-year old Saul indicated "*Mi* blanket *romp,*" the teacher responded, "Oh I see, your blanket is torn." The teacher focused on meaning as opposed to language correctness and used vocabulary relevant to Saul's immediate interest. The teacher validates Saul's language and expands his English vocabulary acquisition through a natural conversation (Alanís et al., 2019). Further, Saul's use of the Spanish word for torn, "*rompió,*" is an example of codeswitching, a natural skill for young bilingual learners.

During reciprocal conversations, adults model the back-and-forth nature of conversational turn-taking by asking questions that encourage children to use their entire language repertoire. Adults who ask questions use rich vocabulary and extend the conversation to scaffold children's language development. This is the case even if the young child is not yet able to respond verbally. Through these reciprocal conversations, educators engage in active listening, smiling, and eye contact, so that children learn to engage with others and value what they have to say (Alanís et al., 2019).

A Responsive Policy Agenda

National, state, and local policies should focus on systemic solutions to inequities in resources for effective language education for young children, especially for young children and families from minoritized communities. These policy measures include (1) healthy child and parental support, (2) economic stability and upward mobility, and (3) accessible and supportive high-quality early care and education (Iruka et al., 2021). Healthy child and parental support policies must provide access to health care and prevention services, preconception and prenatal care, and culturally grounded home visiting programs.

Policies should be actively dismantling inequities and promoting culturally responsive early care and education. Educators need the resources and professional development to promote culturally sustaining policies within programs and inside classrooms that value and leverage the cultural and linguistic assets of children and families. These policies should ensure access to dual language education and inclusive learning environments for all children. It is also critical that the assessments used to judge program quality and assess children's development are culturally valid, reliable, grounded, and sustaining (National Association for the Education of Young Children, 2019). For example, assessments should capture the extent to which children maintain their home language while attaining school language, whether children's oral language skills are being supported through culturally sustaining activities, and how children use their translanguaging skills and varied resources to communicate and make meaning.

Last, EC teacher educators must play a significant role in dismantling inequitable policies and practices. Using their Culturally Efficacious Evolution Model (CEEM), Flores, Claeys, and Gist (2018, p. 31) call for ECEs to engage in a continuous transformative exploration of self and praxis.

CEEM's Five Dimensions

1 Awakening cultural consciousness.
2 Acquiring cultural competence.
3 Developing cultural proficiency.
4 Actualizing cultural and critical responsibility.
5 Realizing cultural efficaciousness.

(Flores, Claeys, & Gist, 2018, pp. 7–9)

This is consistent with the critical conscious cycle that involves "gaining knowledge about the systems and structures that create and sustain inequity (critical analysis), developing a sense of power or capability (sense of agency), and ultimately committing to take action against oppressive conditions (critical action)" (El-Amin et al., 2017, p. 20).

Conclusion

The early years are important for language development as they set the stage for later outcomes and development. Although there are universal aspects of language development, we must understand the sociocultural contexts of language development and the significant influences of key adults and other children at home, in the community, and early care and education settings. Recognizing how language development is impacted by children's sociocultural contexts is critical for ensuring culturally grounded and equitable practices and policies for children and families. Given the changing demographics, ECEs must advocate for equitable environments that incorporate families' cultural and linguistic resources in daily interactions and materials. When educators recognize the strengths of minoritized children and their families, they bring an equity lens to the early care setting. ECEs who are well-versed in relevant research on social and cultural influences for powerful language learning are better positioned to engage in anti-racist, equitable, and inclusive language practices in educational settings to ensure that children realize their full potential.

Closing Reflections

1 Which of the research and theoretical ideas presented in this chapter resonate most deeply with you?
2 What new theory-to-practice connections would you like to implement based upon this chapter's focus on the influence of socialization and culture on language learning for infants and toddlers?

References

Alanís, I., Arreguín, M. G., & Salinas-González, I. (2019). *The essentials: Supporting dual language learners in diverse environments in preschool & kindergarten.* NAEYC.
Alanís, I., & Iruka, I. U. with Friedman, S. (2021). *Advancing equity & embracing diversity in early childhood education: Elevating voices & actions.* NAEYC.

Bronfenbrenner, U., & Morris, P. A. (2007). The bioecological model of human development. In R. M. Lerner (Ed.), *Handbook of child psychology* (pp. 793–828). Wiley. https://doi.org/10.1002/9780470147658.chpsy0114.

Castro, D., & Franco, X (2021). Equitable learning opportunities for young bilingual children. In I. Alanís, I. Iruka, with S. Friedman (Eds.), *Advancing equity and embracing diversity in early childhood education: Elevating voices and actions* (pp. 73–77). NAEYC.

Cui, J., & Natzke, L. (2021). Early childhood program participation: 2019 (NCES 2020–075REV). Retrieved from http://nces.ed.gov/pubsearch/pubsinfo.asp?pubid=2020075REV.

Curenton, S. (2006). Oral storytelling: A cultural art that promotes school readings. *Young Children*, 61(5), 78–89. Retrieved from www.researchconnections.org/childcare/resources/11366.

Cycyk, L. M., & Hammer, C. S. (2020). Beliefs, values, and practices of Mexican immigrant families towards language and learning in toddlerhood: Setting the foundation for early childhood education. *Early Childhood Research Quarterly*, 52, 25–37.

Delgado-Bernal, D. (2001). Learning and living pedagogies of the home: The mestiza consciousness of Chicana students. *International Journal of Qualitative Studies in Education*, 14(5), 623–639.

El-Amin, A., Seider, S., Graves, D., Tamerat, J., Clark, S., Soutter, M., Johannsen, J., & Malhotra, S. (2017). Critical consciousness: A key to student achievement. *Phi Delta Kappan*, 98(5), 18–23.

Farver, J.A.M., Xu, Y., Lonigan, C.J., & Eppe, S. (2013). The home literacy environment and Latino Head Start children's emergent literacy skills. *Developmental Psychology*, 49(4), 775–791.

Flores, B. B., Claeys, L., & Gist C. (2018). *Crafting culturally efficacious teacher preparation and pedagogies*. Lexington Books.

Flores, N., & Rosa, J. (2015). Undoing appropriateness: Raciolinguistic ideologies and language diversity in education. *Harvard Educational Review*, 85, 149171. doi:10.17763/0017-8055.85.2.149.

García, O & Wei, L. (2014). *Translanguaging: Language bilingualism and education*. Palgrave Macmillan.

García Coll, C. T., Lamberty, G., Jenkins, R., McAdoo, H. P., Crnic, K., Wasik, B. H., & García, H. V. (1996). An integrative model for the study of developmental competencies in minority children. *Child Development*, 67(5), 1891–1914. doi:10.1111/j.1467-8624.1996.tb01834.

Gardner-Neblett, N., Pungello, E., & Iruka, I. U. (2012). Oral narrative skills: Implications for the reading development of African American children. *Child Development Perspectives* 6 (3), 218–224. doi:10.1111/j.1750-8606.2011.00225.x.

Guardado, M. (2008). Language, identity and cultural awareness in Spanish-speaking families. *Canadian Ethnic Studies*, 40(3), 171–181. doi:10.1353/ces.2008.0000.

Iruka, I. U., Oliva-Olson, C., & García, E., (2021) *Research to practice brief: Delivering on the promise through equitable polices*. SRI International.

Kibler, A. K., Palacios, N., Paulick, J., & Hill, T. (2020). Languaging among Latinx siblings in immigrant homes: Implications for teaching literacy. *Theory into Practice*, 59(1), 42–52. doi:10.1080/00405841.2019.1665409.

Malmeer, E., & Assadi, N. (2013). Language production and comprehension: The effect of pre-school aged siblings on toddler's language development. *Theory and Practice in Language Studies*, 3(7), 1226–1231.

Markova, G., & Legerstee, M. 2006. Contingency, imitation, and affect sharing: Foundations of infants' social awareness. *Developmental Psychology*, 42(1), 132–141. doi:10.1037/0012-1649.42.1.132.

National Association for the Education of Young Children. (2019). *Advancing equity in early childhood education: A position statement of the National Association for the Education of Young Children*. NAEYC.

National Association for the Education of Young Children. (2020). *Developmentally appropriate practice: A position statement of the National Association for the Education of Young Children*. NAEYC.

National Academies of Sciences, Engineering, and Medicine. (2017). *Promoting the educational success of children and young learning English: Promising futures*. The National Academies Press. https://doi.org/10.17226/24677.

National Institute of Child Health and Human Development Early Child Care Research Network. (2000). The relation of child care to cognitive and language development. *Child Development*, 71, 960980.

Piper, T. (2003). *Language and learning: The home and school years*. Merrill Prentice Hall.

Place, S., & Hoff, E. (2016). Effects and noneffects of input in bilingual environments on dual language skills in 2 ½-year-olds. *Bilingualism: Language and Cognition*, 19(5), 1023–1041. doi:10.1017/S1366728915000322.

Reilly, S. E., Johnson, A. D., Luk, G., & Partika, A. (2020). Head Start classroom features and language and literacy growth among children with diverse language backgrounds. *Early Education and Development*, 31(3), 354–375. doi:10.1080/10409289.2019.1661935.

Rogoff, B. (2003). *The cultural nature of human development*. Oxford University Press.

Ruiz, D. S. (2008). The changing roles of African American grandmothers raising grandchildren: An exploratory study in the Piedmont region of North Carolina. *The Western Journal of Black Studies*, 32(1), 62–71.

Stephens, M. L., Carter-Francique, A. R., & McClain, T. J. (2020). The Black church, an agency for learning, informal religious adult education, and human capital development: A qualitative inquiry into rural African American primary caregiving grandmothers' experiences. *New Horizons in Adult Education & Human Resource Development*, 32(4), 37–49.

Tamis-LeMonda, C. S., Luo, R., McFadden, K. E., Bandel, E. T., & Vallotton, C. (2019). Early home learning environment predicts children's 5th grade academic skills. *Applied Developmental Science*, 23(2), 153–169.

Tamis-LeMonda, C. S., & Song, L. (2012). Parent-infant communicative interactions in cultural context. In R. M. Lerner, E. Easterbrooks, & J. Mistry (Eds.), *Handbook of psychology, volume 6: Developmental psychology* (2nd ed., pp. 143–170). John Wiley & Sons.

Thompson McMillon, G. M., & Edwards, P. A. (2008). Examining shared domains of literacy in the church and school of African American children. In J. Flood, K. B. Heath, & D. Lapp (Eds.), *Handbook of research on teaching literacy through the communicative and visual arts*, Volume II (pp. 319–348). Lawrence Erlbaum. doi:10.13140/2.1.5064.6727.

Torr, J., & Pham, L. (2016). Educator talk in long day care nurseries: How context shapes meaning. *Early Childhood Education Journal*, 44(3), 245–254. doi:10.1007/s10643-015-0705-6.

Trevarthen, C., & Bjørkvold, J. R. (2016). Life for learning: How a young child seeks joy with companions in a meaningful world. In D. Narvaez, J. Braungart-Rieker, L. Miller-Graff, L. Gettler, & P. Hastings (Eds.), *Contexts for young child flourishing: Evolution, family and society* (pp. 28–60). Oxford University Press.

US Census. (2016). Grandparents and grandchildren. September. Retrieved from www.census.gov/newsroom/blogs/random-samplings/2016/09/grandparents-and-grandchildren.html.

US Census. (2018). Older people projected to outnumber children for first time in history. March. Retrieved from www.census.gov/newsroom/press-releases/2018/cb18-41-population-projections.html.

Volk, D., & de Acosta, M. (2004). Mediating networks for literacy learning: The role of Puerto Rican siblings. In E. Gregory, S. Long, & D. Volk (Eds.), *Many pathways to literacy: Young children learning with siblings, grandparents, peers, and communities* (pp. 25–39). Routledge Farmer.

Yosso, T. J. (2005). Whose culture has capital? A critical race theory discussion of community culture of wealth. *Race, Ethnicity, and Education*, 8(1), 69–91. https://doi.org/10.1080/1361332052000341006.

5 Reading for Liberation in Early Childhood

Promoting an Anti-Racist Language and Literacy Curriculum

Patricia Sullivan

Opening Reflections

1 How would you describe your knowledge of anti-racist and liberatory language and literacy education?
2 What questions do you have about applying this approach to working with infants and toddlers?

Anthony is a four-year-old Black boy who stacks books like pancakes. He has two older siblings, one enrolled in the most prestigious public high school in San Francisco and a younger sister, Anita, age two, who thinks she is his twin. Their single mother works for the city and owns her own home, a rarity in a town that spent decades pushing the Black population out. Invisible in one of the most progressive cities in the nation, young Black children like Anthony and Anita face an ecosystem well-versed in the language of equity, but with increased scrutiny this system remains at a loss as to how to educate its Black children. I am a veteran, Black early childhood educator with a doctorate in educational leadership, and I intentionally place liberation and anti-racist education at the heart of my program's language and literacy education for children and families.

Anthony and Anita have been enrolled in my family childcare center for a little more than two years. When I met the pair, Anita was three months old and Anthony was a little more than one. Despite our program's focus on nature and the natural world, and all the time spent on the study of squirrels, bees, and crows in our nearby park, Anthony has consistently selected books with pictures of human faces. Anita is also a social reader, though the book is only part of her process. For both Anthony and Anita, reading is about a lot more than decoding; it's about coming to terms with self, identity, race, racism, gender, and sexism. In this chapter, I describe Anita and Anthony's language and literacy processes, and link their journey to critical ideas about representation of race, ethnicity, gender, and power in children's literature.

Key Idea

For both Anthony and Anita, reading is about a lot more than decoding; it's about coming to terms with self, identity, race, racism, gender, and sexism

DOI: 10.4324/9781003227816-8

Anita's Language and Literacy Process

"Book! Book!" I turn just in time to see the barely walking ten-month-old make her way through the sea of building blocks, metal cars, and puzzles to bring a book that I have read to her several times already that morning. Anita's eyes, as big as her smile, are locked on mine, and I know better than to break the contact, no matter what is happening in the room at that moment. *Just a few more feet*, I think, now aware that a few other children have seen what's happening and have begun digging through the book baskets for their favorites to bring to the reading party that's about to happen. I reach out my arms to grab her and her book before three others race into her path. Anita has picked a popular favorite, but a few of the others are bringing books they just grabbed in their hurry to get to where I sit with Anita.

I always wait until everyone settles down before I begin to read. Actually, I have memorized most of the books they choose. Brown bears, jumping monkeys, a voracious caterpillar and three baby owls later, they drift away one by one, all except Anita. Sitting quietly beside me, she has been waiting for them to leave. She picks up her book and hands it to me again. Finally, it is just us two.

This isn't just Anita's favorite book; this is her favorite book that we share together. It is part of our relationship and although she allows me to read other books from time to time, when she brings me this specific book, I know she wants to snuggle in close, shut out the rest of the world. I've tried to get her excited about other books, particularly books where the main character is a Black girl, but she is steadfast and so I quietly put those books in circulation and read them at story time, and wait for her to notice.

I've had children put my hand on their head so I could gently smooth their hair or grab my legs so that I can't move unless I pick them up. I've even had children fake injuries just to sit in my lap, but Anita is the first in nearly thirty years to invite me to a literary comfort session. I love books, something I think even the youngest children know about me. The evidence is everywhere. We have more books in our classroom library than anything else. We even sacrificed shelf space for games and toys to make space for more books. When I pick up a book, even one I've read a hundred times, I am happy, and that's something that even toddlers can see.

Anthony's Language and Literary Process

Anthony slowly and carefully examines every book on the shelf and in the basket in our classroom library, a laborious procedure. He makes two stacks: one for discards and one for his favorites. This practice became a challenge for me because it requires that Anthony have exclusive access to all the books for several minutes, not to mention the enormous task of reshelving the unwanted books before other children can make their literary choices. Anthony would fuss and cry when I tried to encourage him to take one book at a time and return it before selecting another since he could only "read" one book at a time. When I interfered with his process, he became so upset that he abandoned all the books entirely. Even my attempts to entice him to re-engage by offering to read one of his favorites were unsuccessful.

I realized that while I was trying to encourage his love of books, I was doing just the opposite. So rather than trying to change Anthony's preferred method of engaging with books, I chose to support it by giving him exclusive access to the books while he made his selections, and then asking for his help to reshelve his discard stack before inviting other children to join him. I also gave him his own little basket to hold his selections and transport them to a private corner for a solitary literary experience. The only restrictions

I placed on the books were how the books should be handled and cared for, which Anthony happily complied with. Anthony used to take his favorite books and hide them around the classroom as his own private stash. Once free to make his selections and keep those books for as long as he likes, Anthony no longer needs to hoard his favorites. He reads them and then puts them back in circulation on his own, and when he sees that other children have selected one of those books, he happily sits beside them to enjoy the book with a friend.

"Look! Look!" Anthony excitedly points to the picture of Black Panther, standing on a hilltop overlooking the savanna.

"He is looking for bad guys," his friend explains.

"Here they come!" Anthony shouts, on his feet with both hands over his head. I would never have seen this enthusiastic engagement and book sharing had I not realized that I needed to change how I supported Anthony's literary process. But I found myself with a new question, "Was it the subject (Black Panther), or the experience of seeing Black faces in books that inspired Anthony's literary interests?"

Key Idea

But I found myself with a new question, "Was it the subject (Black Panther), or the experience of seeing Black faces in books that inspired Anthony's literary interests?"

As we reshelved his discard stack, I examined the books that were once his favorites—board books which he now calls "baby books," and books about children learning to use the potty, exploring outer space, or understanding the need to recycle. These books all shared a commonality: none featured a Black child as the main character. I examined all the books in our library, most of which I selected specifically for diversity, and found that while nearly all of them included racially and ethnically diverse faces, only a few told a story from the perspective of Black people or were written by Black authors. I wondered, "Could Anthony's interest in literacy be inspired with more books where the main characters and authors were Black?"

So to deepen my strategies for providing Anita and Anthony with a language and literacy curriculum that placed freedom at its core, I revisited critical literature on representation of culture and identity in children's literature, and the intersectionality of racism and sexuality and Black girl magic.

Representation in Children's Literature Matters

In 1963 *The Snowy Day* became the first Caldecott winner for a children's picture book featuring a Black character. Ezra Jack Keats, the book's author and illustrator, was the son of Jewish Polish immigrants in Brooklyn. Keats was born Jacob Ezra Katz, and it was his experience with anti-Semitism that inspired both his name change and his affinity with other people and cultures facing discrimination. Keats was troubled by the lack of diversity and representation of children of color in his assignments—"None of the manuscripts I'd been illustrating featured any black kids—except for token blacks in the background. My book would have him there simply because he should have been there all along" (Ezra Jack Keats Foundation, 2021a). Keats wasn't the first author to feature a Black child in a children's book, but in a landmark article, *The All-White World of Children's Books*, Nancy Larrick (1965) blasted the children's publishing industry, questioning the deleterious effect of racial erasure—"There is no need to elaborate upon the damage, much of it irreparable, to the Negro child's personality" (p. 63).

Key Idea

When children cannot find themselves reflected in the books they read, or when the images they see are distorted, negative or laughable, they learn a powerful lesson about how they are devalued in the society of which they are a part.

(Bishop, 1990, p. ix)

The Snowy Day was groundbreaking because it broke color barriers. It wasn't a story about being a Black kid, it was about a kid who happened to be Black, experiencing a care-free childhood that Christopher Myers noted in the documentary *Tell Me Another Story*, isn't available to Black and Brown children forced to grow up being "careful" (Ezra Jack Keats Foundation, 2021b). In this film, Debora Taylor, a librarian and activist, said that Black librarians cannot afford to be neutral because children's literature had become a "tool of white supremacy" that has been so effective in its racial erasure of their existence that Black children are not allowed a childhood, "Never loved, never human. That image gets calcified [into American society] over time." After Trevon Martin's murderer was found not guilty, Christopher Myers wrote, "The plethora of threatening images of young Black people has real-life effects" and added, "I wondered: if the man who killed Trevon Martin had read *The Snowy Day* as a kid, would it have been as easy for him to see a seventeen-year-old in a hoodie, pockets full of rainbow candies and sweat tea as a threat?" (Myers, 2013, p. 13).

Christopher Myers and his father Walter Dean Myers (2014) both asked, "Where are all the people of color in children's books?" Walter Dean Myers questioned whether the literacy gap was influenced by the lack of positive representation in children's literature created by children's book publishers. Ebony Elizabeth Thomas (2019) also argues that book publishers are reluctant to increase the percentage of books authored by and about Black people because they believe that the market isn't there; that Black children don't read:

> Maybe it's not that kids and teens of color and other marginalized and minoritized young people don't like to read. Maybe the real issue is that many adults haven't thought very much about the racialized mirrors, windows and doors that are in the books we offer them to read … There has not been much sustained scholarly conversation about how kids and teens of color are affected by their representation in books, movies, comics and online. Nor have previous studies of popular culture critically considered how those story representations shape not only the lives of young people today but whether they will want to pick up the next book.
>
> (Thomas, 2019, p. 7)

Philip Nel (2017) agrees that the lack of representation in children's books is not driven by the market but instead exists as "one of the places where [structural] racism hides" (p. 1), and describes children's literature as a place "where race is displaced, re-coded, hidden" (p. 7). Nel writes that as a white child he never had to wonder if people who looked like him would be in his reading books, and he reminds us that structural racism does not exist for those who don't experience it.

Windows, Mirrors, Sliding Doors, and the Development of Personality

For Rudine Sims Bishop (1990), books are windows into other worlds and cultures and become sliding glass doors where readers can walk through into new worlds. Bishop's explanation of mirrors, however, echoed Larrick's concerns about representation and personality development for children of color:

> Literature transforms human experience and reflects it back to us, and in that reflection, we can see our own lives and experiences as part of the larger human experience. Reading, then, becomes a means of self-affirmation, and readers often seek their mirrors in books.
>
> (Bishop, 1990, p. ix)

As Anthony and Anita develop their language and literacy identities based on cultural and educational experiences and expectations, their personalities will be a blending of how society defines them and how they define themselves. The importance of the first five years of brain development is a familiar refrain in early childhood, but rarely since the Clark Doll Experiments has this critical period included an understanding that brain development includes the development of self-identity and personality. The academy is predictably uninterested in the impact of anti-Black racism on child development or literacy. But if the languages and images in children's literature are truly mirrors, how will Anita and Anthony and other children of Color internalize their limited representation in books and language education? And how can I inspire their love of reading now, before they enter the formal education system where less than half of children of Color read at grade level (California Reading Coalition, 2021)?

The Intersectionality of Racism and Sexism and Black Girl Magic

Anita is innately empathetic. She's almost two now and still constructing her identity. Identifying with and imitating female caregivers in her life engrains the Strong Black Woman stereotype of the selfless nurturer persona as the foundation of her identity. My co-teachers have noted her empathy and dedicated service to other children, but praise from female role models for her thoughtful care of others may limit Anita's perception of who and what she can become. I tell parents how important it is for girls to go into school feeling strong, brave, and smart, so why have I encouraged Anita to adopt this role of selfless caregiver?

Reluctantly, I must admit that it might be because she's so darn good at it. Anita doesn't choose to read books as a solitary activity. For her, books are part of her identity as a caregiver in the classroom. Her favorite reading buddy is Jonathan, a same-age boy with physical disabilities which prevent him from talking, walking, or playing like the other children. Jonathan likes books, especially one board book with a mirror on the last page. Anita enjoys reading this book with Jonathan, holding it for him, turning the pages and checking his facial expressions to make sure he's smiling. While all the other children are kind to Jonathan, he rarely holds their attention for more than a moment. Because Anita understands literacy as a shared experience between caregivers and the cared for, reading with and to Jonathan has become part of her daily play.

Key Idea

Anita will share some of her brother's challenges as a Black person in America, but the intersectionality of gender will deepen those challenges by reinforcing stereotypes specific to Black women that can potentially narrow her vision of herself and limit her life choices.

Anita will share some of her brother's challenges as a Black person in America, but the intersectionality of gender will deepen those challenges by reinforcing stereotypes specific to Black women that can potentially narrow her vision of herself and limit her life choices. Melissa Harris-Perry (2011) exposes and dissects the racial and gender inequity that limits Black women to three stereotyped identities: mammy (caretaker/strong Black woman), Jezebel (over-sexualized/welfare queen) and Sapphire (angry/sassy/loud).

> The strong Black woman is easily recognizable. She confronts all trials and tribulations. She is a source of unlimited support for her family. She is a motivated, hardworking breadwinner. She is always prepared to do what needs to be done for her family and her people. She is sacrificial and smart. She suppresses her emotional needs while anticipating those of others.
>
> (Harris-Perry, 2011, p. 21)

While Anita may be too young to recognize the strong Black woman persona, she already understands the acceptability of that role in her family and at school, which is likely to emerge as her preferred social identity. Although the strong Black woman persona may superficially appear to be positive; it glorifies the erasure of self for Black girls, assigning to them the role of "mule, carrying the weight of racial prejudice and gendered inequity" (Harris-Perry, 2011, p. 6.) Anita will fall into the under-researched intersection of racism and sexism where targeted interventions, either by race or gender, fail to support the unique challenges faced by Black girls (Ricks, 2014). To expand Anita's self-concept, I have introduced more books that feature Black girls in nontraditional roles such as artists, ballerinas, astronauts, mathematicians, pilots, and politicians. This effort aligns with social media #BlackGirlMagic, which has inspired Black girls all over the world to see themselves as unique and special, showcasing their invisible contributions.

The Summer of Racial Reckoning and Black Child Literacy

Anti-Black bias was front page news in 2020 as the nation focused momentarily on the blatant disregard for Black people and the more than four thousand hate crimes against Black Americans (US Department of Justice, 2020). In an effort to disrupt the preschool to prison pipeline, San Francisco was one of the few cities where legislators voted to reallocate a fraction of the multimillion dollar police budget to the Black community and programs developed to support home libraries for Black children. Anthony is one of the children who has received books from San Francisco's Dreamkeepers Initiative and has begun to build his own library of books by authors of color. Like the National Black Child Development Institute's *Read to Succeed* program, Dreamkeepers supports and funds Black children's access to representational literature. But in the 2021 NBCDI national conference, Black educators and academics insisted that more needs to be done to help public school teachers and parents work together to inspire Black literacy, Black representation in books, Black authors, and a demand for more Black faces at the executive level of children's publishing. As Horning (2014) argues:

> If we want to see change, if we want to see more diversity in literature, we have to buy the books. Buy them for our schools, for our libraries, for our families, for our friends. We must be the agents of change. Otherwise, we are all participants in the "cultural lobotomy." And it won't be technology that threatens the very existence of books. It'll be their complete and utter irrelevance in the real world that never was and never will be all white.
>
> (Horning, 2014, para. 16)

Reframing Anthony and Anita's worldview in the context of systemic racism within the education system requires an intentional and unrelenting resistance to what Bettina Love (2019) calls the soul murder of Black children. Through counternarratives that battle stereotypes and increase representation in language and literacy education to reflect the contributions of Black people and Black culture, I hope that these children develop a worldview that includes not only a positive image of Black people, but inspired predictions of their own contributions to the world.

Language and literacy experts recommend that teachers reduce their dependence on boring culturally insensitive books, allow more freedom of choice in literacy materials, and bring back silent reading time in classrooms (Education Week Spotlight, 2021). I want to implement these goals and strategies to prepare Anita and Anthony for a school system that will have little time or patience for their quirky literary processes. If these Black children can develop foundational language and literacy knowledge and skills before they enter formal schooling, they will have a much better chance of academic achievement in the primary grades and beyond. They will also demonstrate to kindergarten teachers who don't expect Black children to start school with the ability to read that Black literacy is real.

Black children need to see themselves positively represented in an American culture where the mere suggestion that their lives matter is controversial, where White fragility is more important than social justice, and where anti-Black racism is the deepest well. Most early childhood educators are well versed in the importance of the first three years of human brain development as fundamental to lifelong learning, but rarely do we discuss how these same years are critical in the development of self-identity and racial literacy. When placed within the context of a society and an education system rife with racial inequities, as educators we must ask ourselves how we can ensure that all children, especially Black children, see themselves as intellectual beings, competent learners and scholars who can slam dunk algebraic logic, high hurdle a hate-filled history of American citizenship and cakewalk through new technologies just beginning to recognize the creative contributions of Black people and Black culture, languages, and literacies.

> We build our temples for tomorrow, strong as we know how, and we stand on top of the mountain, free within ourselves.
>
> (Hughes, 1926)

Closing Reflections

1 How has Patricia's work with Anita and Anthony deepened your knowledge of practical ways to support young children's language and literacy learning as aligned with their personal and cultural identities?
2 How might you implement certain aspects of Patricia's ideas for promoting anti-racist and liberatory language and literacy education in your professional work?

References

Bishop, R. S. (1990). Mirrors, windows and sliding glass doors. *Perspectives: Choosing and using books for the classroom*, 6 (3), ix–xi.

California Reading Coalition. (2021). California reading report card. Retrieved from www.careads.org/reportcard.

Education Week Spotlight. (2021). Literacy in education. *Education Week*, June 15.

Ezra Jack Keats Foundation. (2021a). Ezra's life. Retrieved from www.ezra-jack-keats.org/ezras-life.

Ezra Jack Keats Foundation. (2021b). Tell me another story: Diversity in children's literature. [Video]. Retrieved from https://youtu.be/BNry9keQcfI.

Harris-Perry, M. (2011). *Sister citizen: Shame, stereotypes, and Black women in America*. Yale University Press.

Horning, K. (2014). Children's books: Still an all-white world? *School Library Journal*, May 1. Retrieved from www.slj.com/?detailStory=childrens-books-still-an-all-white-world.

Hughes, L. (1926). The Negro artist and the racial mountain. *Nation*, 122.

Larrick, N. (1965). The all-white world of children's books. *Saturday Review*, 11, 63–65.

Love, B. (2019). *We want to do more than survive: Abolitionist teaching and the pursuit of educational freedom*. Beacon Press.

Myers, C. (2013). Young dreamers. *The Horn Book*, 89 (6), 10–14.

Myers, W. D. & Myers, C. (2014). Where are the people of color in children's books? *The New York Times*, March 15. Retrieved from www.nytimes.com/2014/03/16/opinion/sunday/where-are-the-people-of-color-in-childrens-books.html.

Nel, P. (2017). *Was the Cat in the Hat Black? The hidden racism of children's literature and the need for diverse books*. Oxford.

Ricks, S. (2014). Falling through the cracks: Black girls and education. *Interdisciplinary Journal of Teaching and Learning*, 4(1), 10–21.

Thomas, E. B. (2019). *The dark fantastic: Race and the imagination from Harry Potter to the Hunger Games*. New York University Press.

US Department of Justice. (2020). Uniform crime report: Hate crime statistics, 2019. Retrieved from https://ucr.fbi.gov/hate-crime/2019/topic-pages/victims.

6 Expanding Language and Literacy Opportunities for Children with Disabilities

Jennifer M. Ventura

Opening Reflections

1 How do you feel about your knowledge base for understanding and supporting children with developmental and language disabilities and delays?
2 What is working well in terms of your creation and implementation of inclusive developmental and language learning environments, and which areas would you like to strengthen?

Introduction

In this chapter, I share strategies for effectively mentoring and coaching educators who support infants and toddlers with disabilities or who have developmental delays. My discussion is based on my past work in the field and my current role as a Bilingual Spanish and English Developmental Inclusion Specialist. I especially highlight the role of culturally responsive language and early literacy education for these children, their teachers, and their families. I also discuss assessment measures and teaching approaches designed to strengthen play, social interaction, and communicative skills for children with disabilities.

I base my work supporting teachers in inclusive settings on a definition that identifies key components of high-quality inclusive programs:

> Early childhood inclusion embodies the values, policies, and practices that support the right of every infant and young child and his or her family, regardless of ability, to participate in a broad range of activities and contexts as full members of families, communities, and society. The desired results of inclusive experiences for children with and without disabilities and their families include a sense of belonging and membership, positive social relationships and friendships, and development and learning to reach their full potential. The defining features of inclusion that can be used to identify high-quality early childhood programs and services are access, participation, and supports.
>
> (Division for Early Childhood and the National Association for the Education of Young Children, 2009, p. 2)

DOI: 10.4324/9781003227816-9

Key Idea

The defining features of inclusion that can be used to identify high-quality early childhood programs and services are access, participation, and supports.
(Division for Early Childhood and the National Association for the Education of Young Children, 2009, p. 2)

This perspective serves to unite educators nationally for raising awareness and deepening knowledge of inclusive goals and practices for all children and families. It helps us view language and literacy education for all children, regardless of developmental needs and talents, as a human "right" to become "full members of families, communities, and society." The definition also highlights the critical elements of "access, participation, and supports," which form the foundation for high-quality language and literacy opportunities for all children.

It is critical, also, that we conceptualize and implement developmentally appropriate language and literacy practices emphasizing the talents, interests, and needs of all children:

> Educators are prepared to individualize their teaching strategies to meet the specific needs of individual children, including children with disabilities and children whose learning is advanced, by building on their interests, knowledge, and skills. Educators use all the strategies identified here and consult with appropriate specialists and the child's family; they see that the child gets the adaptations and specialized services needed for full inclusion as a member of the community and that no child is penalized for their ability status.
> (National Association for the Education of Young Children, 2022, p. xliii)

Key Idea

A definition of early childhood inclusion should help create high expectations for every child, regardless of ability, to reach his or her full potential.
(Division for Early Childhood and the National Association for the Education of Young Children, 2009, p. 3)

An overall commitment, then, to full inclusion emphasizes viewing education as a human right for all children, acquiring deep knowledge and expertise in culturally and linguistically responsive practices, and ensuring equitable educational access to high-quality education for children from historically marginalized communities.

The Role of Inclusion Specialists

Increasingly, young children aged 0–5 spend six to eight hours a day under the care of early childhood educators in varied educational settings. As educators, we play important roles in supporting the cultural, social, cognitive, physical, and linguistic needs and talents of our youngest children with disabilities. My current position as a Bilingual

Spanish and English Developmental Inclusion Specialist in San Francisco, California, has granted me the opportunity to work with early childhood educators and leaders to implement inclusion practices in early childhood settings. In coaching and mentoring early childhood educators, I introduce and guide the integration of effective environments, materials, and strategies to maximize the full range of opportunities for participation and learning of children with an identified diagnosis or with developmental delays. The primary responsibility in my work involves helping teachers to strengthen their toolbox of ideas, approaches, and strategies for understanding and supporting bilingual children of Color and their families in inclusion settings.

I have worked in a range of early childhood settings and capacities, which has afforded me different insights into understanding how the environment, interventions, and collaboration with families and specialists play an important role when meeting the needs of children with disabilities and developmental delays. I have also worked with other inclusion specialists who work with teachers and children with disabilities and their families, and it is helpful for all educators and families to learn about the roles and responsibilities of these specialists, and how their work connects with children's multilingual and multiliteracy literacy learning (Table 6.1).

These specialists use certain diagnostic and assessment tools and strategies for supporting educators in a range of settings, direct support for children, and advice and care for families of children with disabilities.

Having first-hand experience as a teacher and also receiving mentoring from coaches and specialists at my previous work, I understand the range of situations that can challenge educators when learning new strategies and learning to support children whose needs may be unfamiliar. The educators whom I now coach often ask questions that focus on children's diagnoses and how to engage children in activities to support their individual needs in classrooms. I have learned as a teacher and coach that our ongoing efforts to deepen our knowledge of children's individual needs is the most valuable approach for the long-term support of children with disabilities.

Screening and Diagnostic Tools

Effective screening tools provide teachers, coaches, inclusion specialists, and families with important information for understanding children's individual talents, strengths, preferences, and needs. It is critical that all professionals and family members work together to share and use information gathered from both home and educational settings to establish, implement, and monitor a plan to support children with disabilities. For the educators whom I mentor and coach at publicly funded centers, they are required to use certain assessment measures for diagnosis and documentation. While I take a critical stance toward assessments regarding the cultural and linguistic relevancy of these assessments for multilingual children of Color with disabilities and delays, these measures are mandated and part of the centers' funding streams and policies.

Ages and Stages Questionnaire

I work with local programs and educators to implement the Ages and Stages Questionnaire (ASQ-3), a questionnaire that enables families to share their observations and insights about their children's development and any concerns about their children's development (https://agesandstages.com). Although there are few effective screening and informational tools for families of children with disabilities, they help families share

Table 6.1 Professionals who support inclusive environments and children's language and literacy learning

Roles	Description	Language Connections
Teacher of the Deaf and Hard of Hearing	• A special education teacher trained to teach Deaf and hard of hearing students. TODHHs address unique language needs and the academic impact of those language needs.	• Teach various skills that include expressive and receptive language, self-advocacy, literacy, and many other skills to meet students' needs.
Early Childhood Special Educator (ECSE)	• Creates an individual education plan (IEP) for children 3 and older with development delays and diagnosed disabilities. • Created within interdisciplinary teams in which one member is the ECSE.	• Provides support and works on Individualize Family Service Plan (IFSP) that focuses on different areas of support depending on the child's needs. The focus can be on language and communication.
Early Childhood Intervention Specialist	• Supports children with developmental delays and diagnosed challenges from birth to age 3 and their families. • Works closely with families to assist with accessing services such as preschool and childcare.	• Provides support and works on Individualize Family Service Plan (IFSP) that focuses on different areas of support depending on the child's needs. The focus can be on language and communication.
Speech and Language Specialist; Speech and Language and Feeding Specialist	• Assesses, diagnoses, and supports children with a range of disabilities to ensure educational development in a range of settings.	• Specific strategies to support children with disabilities with a range of language and literacy needs.
Child Life Specialist	• Supports young children through various interventions such as emotional support, medical play, developmental play, and other play forms.	• Supports children's language and literacy needs regarding new or existing medical and educational diagnoses.
Occupational Therapist	• Focuses on fine motor, eye-hand coordination, and day-to-day tasks, which may include gross motor tasks such as dressing.	• Supports a child's ability to inhibit impulse control e.g. regulate their body, interrupting during conversations and help the child to plan an organize their thoughts to be able to respond.
TVI, teacher of the visually impaired and also teacher of blind and low-vision students	• TVIs work with students birth-22 and provide direct and consultive special education services specific to the impact of vision impairment (including Deafblindness) on a child's learning and development. They also implement accessible educational media and collaborate with other therapists for effective adaptations.	• Conducts assessment and direct instruction of the Expanded Core Curriculum (ECC), which addresses the unique learning needs of blind and low vision students. Also facilitates low and nonvisual access to the primary curriculum including communication, literacy and numeracy objectives.

Roles	Description	Language Connections
Certified Orientation and Mobility Specialist (COMS)	• COMS teach blind and low vision individuals (including Deafblindness) how to travel safely and independently in their environments. They work with students of all ages from infancy through adulthood.	• Provides blind, low vision, and Deafblind students with a set of foundational skills to use residual visual, auditory, and other sensory information to understand and engage with their environments. Also supports children's ECC-related needs.

valuable information for educators. The ASQ-3 is designed to screen for possible developmental delays and not for children who may already have a diagnosis, and the ASQ-3 is suitable for children aged one month to 5 years. This is a multilingual tool that focuses in part on language and communication knowledge. For example, one item asks families, "Does your child tell you at least two things about common objects? For example, if you say to your child, "Tell me about your ball," does she say something like, "It's round. I throw it. It's big"? The developmental scores for this and all items are "yes," "sometimes," "not yet."

Individualized Family Support Plan

For families with children with an already identified diagnosis, they receive an Individualized Family Support Plan (IFSP) that will support with individual interventions from birth to three years of age (Center for Parent Information & Resources, undated). This is a foundational document and plan for families to ensure comprehensive services and support for children with disabilities, and a range of inclusion specialists often work with families to implement and monitor the IFSP. The plan includes information such as children's current developmental talents and needs, family information, expected outcomes, and specific intervention services—all of which can feature language and literacy goals, materials, and strategies.

Desired Results Developmental Profile

The Desired Results Developmental Profile (DRDP) (California Department of Education, Early Education and Support Division, 2010) is designed for early infancy through kindergarten, and is available in multiple languages. The DRDP allows educators to share their objective observations and to document children's learning and development three times a year across a range of developmental domains. The language and literacy development section focuses on receptive language, responsiveness to language, reciprocal communication and conversation, and interest in literacy. For example, the receptive language element for infants and toddlers features a developmental continuum of 9 ministages of mastery. These include stage 1 of "responding earlier" (e.g. child turns head or looks in the direction of a voice), stage 5 of "exploring later" (e.g. child gets jacket after an adult says, "Get your jacket. It's time to go outside."), to the 9th and final stage of "Integrating earlier" (e.g. explains how to plant seeds to a peer after an adult reads a book about planting seeds).

   In my work with teachers, I reference the ASQ-4 and DRDP results and the IFSP's goals to plan caregiving, instruction, and holistic support for children.

Inclusion Approaches and Supporting Language Learning

Teachers often share that they are not sure which strategies to implement when children are not vocalizing, imitating sounds, or verbally and nonverbally communicating. Meeting the social and language needs of a group of children as well as individual children with disabilities requires careful planning, implementation, dialogue, teamwork, and reflection. I have found that I best support this daily work in connection with how teachers construct opportunities for language learning, play, and social interaction.

Play and Environments

Chapters 1–3 of this book specifically focus on play, interaction, and language. I define play as the way in which children express who they are, show their interests and abilities, and reveal to us their individual developmental progression. In terms of applying this view for understanding and supporting the language growth of children with disabilities, we must support all children's individual skills and abilities. The environment plays a part in the experiences children encounter each day. It is critical that we intentionally design the physical environment to feature the space, materials, and equipment to support all children's developmental and communicative talents social interactions with peers and adults. We can also link the physical environment with the temporal environment, which involves carefully considering the length and sequence of routines and activities that we present to all children. In inclusive environments, routines and activities have permeable and flexible participation boundaries so that children can enter play and communicate at their own pace.

Universal Design for Learning

The Universal Design for Learning (UDL) framework helps us conceptualize and utilize strategies to understand and support children who may need adaptations or modifications to the environment. Universal Design for Learning also takes into account the cultural, linguistic and ability diversity of all children (Gargiulo & Metcalf, 2016; Schuman, 2017). UDL is based on three principles that provide multiple means of:

1   *Presentation*—a variety of ways for children to acquire, process and integrate information, knowledge, and skills.
2   *Expression*—a variety of ways to show what children are learning.
3   *Engagement*—various opportunities for children to be motivated and challenged.

The framework reminds us to look beyond the physical environment and provide an inclusive environment in all learning areas that ensures access, participation, and support for diverse learners.

Universal Design for Learning (UDL) Principles

1   *Presentation*—a variety of ways for children to acquire, process and integrate information, knowledge, and skills.
2   *Expression*—a variety of ways to show what children are learning.
3   *Engagement*—various opportunities for children to be motivated and challenged.

Observe, Wait and Listen

Observe, Wait and Listen (OWL) is an effective strategy to consider during interactions and supporting language opportunities for all children (Tomlin, Sturm, & Koch, 2009). Observe is defined as focusing one's attention on children to notice what they are interested in or trying to communicate. As educators, we are at times more often looking for evidence of children's oral language rather than nonverbal communication. We must be aware that some children are subtle in the ways they express themselves, and when we observe closely, we can notice what they are trying to communicate.

Wait refers to giving children the opportunity to initiate communication with peers and adults. This part of the OWL approach is easier said than done in my own experience, as waiting involves patience on our part; we are accustomed to initiating language and interaction with children and moving along at a pace that we have predetermined meets our schedule. Listening, the third OWL component, involves paying close attention to what children are saying and trying to communicate in whatever manner and mode they are using. For children with the skill to vocalize either sounds, pseudo words, or conventional words, we might be more apt to feel that we can listen to what they are communicating. For children with the skill to communicate nonverbally, either through nonverbal means and/or adaptive technology, we must listen with care to respond with the supportive intentionality to engage with the children.

Watch, Ask and Adapt

The strategy of Watch, Ask and Adapt is adapted from the WestEd Program for Infant/ Toddler Care (Lally, Mangione, & Greenwald, D., 2006). Watch refers to watching for both verbal and non-verbal cues. Ask does not refer to asking children questions, but rather to ask oneself what message children are sending, and to consider their emotional, intellectual, and physical needs at a certain moment, which might be related to hunger or other emotions. If children can verbally communicate, asking children directly can provide us with more information of what they are trying to say.

Face to Face Communication

One way that we can slow down and provide effective inclusive language interactions involves face-to-face body positioning, which has been discussed in Chapter 3 and other chapters in this book. For children who need to learn and communicate at their own pace, face-to-face communication is an effective strategy for conversation as well as when we are reading, singing, dancing, or showing an object. We can utilize this strategy by sitting on the floor while children sit in small chairs. When interacting with an infant, laying on our stomach as children sit, lie, and move on the floor encourages face to face communication. For children who need special seats or mobile devices, we can move ourselves into closer contact with children, and help other children move into new physical positions to interact with peers with mobility challenges.

Follow Children's Leads

How many times have you or another child invited a child to play, and they join only for a moment or not at all? Sometimes, children can be so engaged in what they are doing that they are not interested in stopping. However, when we follow the child's lead, we pick up on their interests and not our interests and goals. In terms of providing language opportunities, following children's leads shows us not only what children know but how they learn. We sometimes tend to focus on what children can't do, but when we can extend their language by imitating children's sounds and words and nonverbal communication, we convey to children that what and how they communicate matters. When we comment on children's initiations we also let children know we are paying attention. It is also helpful to consider how our verbal feedback conveys our commitment to following our children's leads.

Strategy: SSCAN

Infants and toddlers with certain developmental and language challenges may interact less in small and large group settings. As mentioned earlier, if children have limited verbal skills, we may miss their subtle attempts at social and communicative initiation. In addition, children who are dual language learners may not fully understand everything that their peers and adults say as they are learning English. I have found that SSCAN is an effective strategy for providing opportunities for infants and toddlers during daily classroom routines (Weitzman & Greenberg, 2002, p. 153).

SSCAN Elements

Small groups are best
Set up an appropriate activity
Carefully observe each child's level of participation and interaction
Adapt your response to each child's needs
Now keep it going

During my mentoring of infant-toddler educators, we reflect on when are the best times to have small groups. Once the educator has identified specific times in the day, we then begin to implement the SSCAN process. We often need to tinker with specifics of the SSCAN process depending on the particular environment and children involved, and we rely on continued observation, documentation, and reflection to make subsequent changes.

Closing Thoughts

In this chapter, I discussed key factors that are foundational for working with infants and toddlers with disabilities or developmental delays. When we effectively implement universal design for learning (UDL) and other approaches described in this chapter, we provide inclusive opportunities for language and literacy access, participation, and support for all children. While the ideas, approaches, and language strategies discussed in this chapter are not new to our field, we do need additional training and support for learning how these ideas and practices can support children with disabilities in a range of settings and over long periods of time. While there are other strategies that I am sure you implement in your classroom that were not mentioned in this chapter, I hope that reading this chapter has sparked and invited you to consider additional ways to understand and support the language learning of all of your children. I also encourage you to initiate and deepen your collaboration with colleagues, inclusion specialists, and children's families to create and sustain inclusive language and literacy environments and approaches for all children.

Closing Reflections

1   Which of the ideas, assessments, approaches, and strategies that Jennifer presented in this chapter would you like to adapt in your inclusion work with children, families, and colleagues? Which elements might you implement in the short-term, and which ones might you wait on?

2   What additional professional resources and support do you need to make these changes? How might you reach out to colleagues and families as you embark on this process?

References

California Department of Education, Early Education and Support Division. (2010). *Desired results developmental profile*. California Department of Education, Early Education and Support Division.

Center for Parent Information & Resources. Undated. Writing the IFSP for your child. Retrieved from www.parentcenterhub.org/ifsp.

Cunconan-Lahr, R. L., & Stifel, S. (2013). *Universal Design for Learning (UDL) checklist for early childhood environments*. North Community College and Pennsylvania Developmental Disabilities Council.

Division for Early Childhood and the National Association for the Education of Young Children. (2009). *Early childhood inclusion: A joint position statement of the Division for Early Childhood (DEC) and the National Association for the Education of Young Children (NAEYC)*. National Association for the Education of Young Children.

Gargiulo, R. M., & Metcalf, D. (2016). *Teaching in today's inclusive classrooms: A universal design for learning approach*. Cengage Learning.

Lally, J. R., Mangione, P. L., & Greenwald, D. (Eds.).(2006). Concepts for care: 20 essays on infant/toddler development and learning. WestEd.

National Association for the Education of Young Children. (2019). *Advancing equity in early childhood education: A position statement of the National Association for the Education of Young Children*. National Association for the Education of Young Children.

National Association for the Education of Young Children. (2022). *Developmentally appropriate practice in early childhood programs: Serving children from birth through age 8*. National Association for the Education of Young Children.

Schuman, H. (2017). Self-and peer evaluation in inclusive ECEC Settings. Retrieved from www.ogretmenplatform.org/subOutputs/subOutput4.pdf.

Tomlin, A. M., Sturm, L., & Koch, S. M. (2009). Observe, listen, wonder, and respond: A preliminary exploration of reflective function skills in early care providers. *Infant Mental Health Journal: Official Publication of The World Association for Infant Mental Health*, 30(6), 634–647.

Weitzman, E., & Greenberg, J. (2002). *Language learning and loving it: A guide to promoting children's social, language, and literacy development in early childhood centers* (2nd edition). Hanen Centre.

Part III
Multilingualism

7 Bilingual First Language Acquisition

What the Research Says

Annick De Houwer

Opening Reflections

1   Consider your current and/or previous training on bilingualism and multilingualism. Which theories, ideas, and practices resonate most deeply with you, and what new knowledge are you seeking in this area?
2   If you work with or know young children and families from multilingual backgrounds, what challenges and talents do you see in their multilingual learning?

Young Children Learning More Than a Single Language

A Short History

The scientific study of young children learning to speak more than a single language began in the early 1900s. The initial focus of this first exclusively European research was on individual children but starting in the 1930s group studies emerged, first in the United States and later elsewhere. Relatively few scholars globally, however, studied early bilingual development. It took nearly 100 years before there was enough collective knowledge to warrant publishing textbooks on the subject, written by North American scholars (Genesee, Paradis, & Crago, 2004) and myself, a European one (De Houwer, 2009). Both books emphasized the wide range of variation among bilingual children and the importance of children's language learning environments, which consist of the speech children hear (their language input) and the social contexts for language use. Social contexts include first and foremost children's immediate family and anyone else regularly interacting with children in the home context, and they may include family external group settings such as day centers and preschools. All those social contexts communicate to children whether a particular language is valued.

Contemporary research has benefited from an ever-increasing sophistication in research methods and from the creation of international cooperative networks among scholars working on bilingual development (see e.g. De Houwer, 2021). The twenty-first century has also seen a new focus on bilingual children's well-being: In 2006 I proposed that researchers pay attention to what I have called Harmonious Bilingual Development, or the development of two languages in the absence of negative feelings associated with a bilingual setting, where families use more than a single language in their personal lives. Recent reviews (De Houwer, 2020; Hollebeke et al., 2020; Müller et al., 2020) show a steady increase in studies about factors supporting Harmonious Bilingualism for all

DOI: 10.4324/9781003227816-11

members of families who find themselves in a bilingual setting. There is also increased interest from early care and education practitioners in how to support bilingual children in their development. Interest has likely been spurred on by the ever more visible (and audible!) presence of young bilingual children in our educational institutions. Probably a fifth to a third of children in "Western" countries where schools teach in a single societal language grow up with that language in addition to another language they hear at home (De Houwer, 2021, p. 4).

Most Bilingual Children Hear Two Languages in the Home

Often people assume that bilingual children hear one language at home, and another at daycare or preschool. In reality, an estimated three quarters of bilingually raised children hear *both* the school language and another language at home, rather than *just* another language than the school language (De Houwer, 2021). Early bilingualism, then, typically concerns children who hear two languages from birth in the home. They are learning their languages in a Bilingual First Language Acquisition (BFLA) setting (De Houwer, 2009) and have two first languages, Language A and Language Alpha. This notation of translated versions of the first letter of the alphabet (proposed by Wölck 1987/1988) means there is no first or second language—both languages are first.

BFLA children have no experience with monolingualism and differ from children who start off hearing a single language at home but later start hearing the societal language at daycare or preschool. These emergent bilingual children grow up in an Early Second Language Acquisition (ESLA) setting, and have a first and a second language (Genesee et al., 2004). Their developmental trajectories are quite different from those of BFLA children, at least in the first 6 years of life (De Houwer, 2021). This chapter focuses on critical dimensions of bilingual learning for BFLA children in the first 5 years of life.

Bilingual? Multilingual?

So far I have only referred to bilingualism and children learning two languages. Many children, though, learn more than two languages. However, the research on trilingual or quadrilingual children is still very limited. What we know from children's development involving two languages seems to apply to children with more than two languages as well. In this sense, the terms bilingualism and multilingualism are synonyms.

Developmental Trajectories for BFLA Children in Infancy

The BFLA Setting at Home

A BFLA setting is created when newborn babies start to regularly hear two languages at home from their caregiver(s). I introduce five firstborn newborns to you that we will follow throughout the rest of the chapter. They are fictional children but you can find real, live versions of them as described in the scientific literature and as present in many YouTube videos. Some are inspired by the consultancy work I have been doing with parents from all over the world over four decades.

Our first newborn is Kimmy. Kimmy was born in the USA to a mother from Korea and a father from Ohio. Kimmy's parents speak English among each other but once Kimmy was born her mother found she could not but address her in Korean—it felt so strange to speak English to a newborn, and, besides, Kimmy's Korean grandparents do not speak English, so Korean is really important for Kimmy's family. Kimmy's father does not understand Korean. Kimmy started attending an English-speaking day care center after three months.

Let's meet Pedro. Pedro was also born in the USA, to bilingual parents with Mexican roots who speak both Spanish and English with each other and who each started speaking both Spanish and English to Pedro. Pedro didn't attend any day care center and both his parents spent a lot of time with him in his first two years.

Marie was born in Edmonton, Canada. Her mother is French-Canadian and has many relatives in Quebec. Her father is English-Canadian but understands French. Prior to Marie's birth her parents decided they would each speak just one language at home—they were already using dual language conversations with each other, where Marie's mother spoke French and her father English. Now they would only use those kinds of conversations with each other, and each speak their own first language to Marie. Marie started attending a small French-English day care after six months.

Further afield we find Hiroko, who was born to a Japanese mother and an American father in Japan. Hiroko's parents speak English to each other, and although Hiroko's father understands some Japanese he is hesitant to use it, and decided to speak English to his daughter. Hiroko's mother found it natural to speak Japanese to her daughter but continued speaking mainly English to her husband. Hiroko's father is a freelance writer and can spend a lot of time with his family at home. Her mother has a profession that does not allow her to spend that much time at home.

Finally, we meet Einar. His mother emigrated to Germany from Norway 15 years earlier and speaks fluent German (as well as Norwegian, Danish, and English). She does not have a live-in partner but wants Einar to be able to communicate with her relatives and friends in Norway. She also wants him to speak German before he arrives at preschool, because she is aware of the communicative problems many children have when they attend a preschool where at first they do not understand or speak the language. She thus decided to speak both Norwegian and German to Einar from the very start, and found herself singing Norwegian songs and telling Norwegian stories to Einar but using German when giving him a bath or showing him around the house. Because of generous maternity leave conditions, she devoted herself entirely to Einar in his first year of life.

Tuning in to Two Languages from the Start

Like all BFLA babies, Korean/English-hearing Kimmy distinguished between the sounds of her two input languages early on (see e.g. Sundara, 2022). Simultaneously, like many BFLA babies, Kimmy learned to associate different kinds of sounds with different people. One time Kimmy's mother came to pick up Kimmy from the day care and inadvertently addressed her in English. Kimmy, then seven months old, looked at her mother with a puzzled expression and started to cry: she was expecting to hear Korean sounds from her mother. Einar, on the other hand, was quite happy with his mother speaking either Norwegian or German to him. After all, he had been used to that from the start. When he was eight months old, he could understand words in both languages. Some BFLA babies first show understanding in just one of the languages as Hiroko first showed comprehension of some English words but not of Japanese. After her mother spent more time reading Japanese books with Hiroko, though, Hiroko soon caught up in Japanese.

It is typical for BFLA infants to understand more words in one language than the other. They understand a lot more words than monolingual peers (De Houwer, 2021), which may be related to the fact that BFLA infants understand many words in both languages that are translations of each other. Thus, for instance, Pedro understood both Spanish "perro" and English "dog."

Starting to Talk

Marie's parents were overjoyed when they heard her say something that sounded like "mama" at the age of ten months. They weren't sure, though, whether this was an attempt at English "mommy" or French "maman." Indeed, with BFLA infants it is often difficult to say which language a word-like form belongs to—infants are just starting to learn to say sounds and combine them.

It takes a few years until children (whether bilingual or monolingual) can pronounce words correctly. In the meantime, they do build up their vocabulary. Familiar people can recognize these words, even if they sound a bit strange (like "nana" for banana, or "efan" for elephant). Scholars therefore ask people familiar with a particular child to report on the child's vocabulary. Based on such reports and recordings of child speech, scientists have discovered that BFLA infants and toddlers say words from both languages from around age 13 months.

The number of words said in each language rapidly increases across the second year of life. Individual BFLA children may say similar or different numbers of words in each language. There are also large differences among BFLA children in how many words they can say at a particular age. For instance, by 22 months Einar could say a total of 1,000 words (Norwegian and German combined), whereas Kimmy had 400 words by then (English and Korean combined). 400 words is still quite a bit, but why was there a 600-word difference between Einar and Kimmy? As reviewed by Head Zauche et al. (2017), how much and in what way caregivers interact with young children helps us understand such differences among children. Einar's mother was very talkative and described everything she was doing with Einar. She stayed at home in his first year and took every opportunity to verbally engage with Einar. She used highly exaggerated, sing-song ways of talking to him in the first months that he simply loved and that drew his attention to her mouth. Later she encouraged his own talking by asking questions, and never failed to name things he pointed to. She started to read books with him early on. Kimmy's parents were much less talkative, and Kimmy spent a lot of time in day care, where there was little time for one-on-one interaction. Book reading at home was a once-a-week event, if it happened at all. Although Kimmy did say about 50 words in Korean, her English vocabulary was far greater (350). This difference reflects the fact that she spent far more time in an English- than a Korean-speaking environment. The number of words toddlers say is an important predictor of how well and how fast they will be able to build sentences. In monolingual children, vocabulary size at age two predicts later academic achievement (Head Zauche et al., 2017).

Developmental Trajectories for BFLA Children in Early Childhood

Words

After his second birthday, Pedro preferred to talk about food in Spanish and about games and cartoons in English. Such lexical specialization is typical of BFLA children: they tend to talk about some things in only one of their languages. This does not keep them from also having overlapping vocabulary, where they refer to the same thing in each language. For instance, Hiroko knew both the Japanese and English words for the family's many rooftop garden plants. She loved plants and both her parents did, too, so they taught her all the names in each language. Words by themselves are not enough, though; they need to be combined into sentences.

Sentences

By their second birthday, BFLA toddlers combine two or more words into short sentences, mostly combining words from the same language (unilingual utterances) but also occasionally words from both languages (mixed utterances). As utterances become longer, they become more complex.

In unilingual utterances (with words from just a single language), BFLA children use the word order and other grammatical elements from the same language as the words. They do this in each language. This is evidence for the Separate Development Hypothesis, which states that the morphosyntactic development of one language in BFLA does not systematically affect the morphosyntactic development of the other (e.g. De Houwer, 2009). Furthermore, the structure of most of BFLA children's unilingual utterances strongly resembles that of utterances used by monolingual peers. One of BFLA children's languages may be far better developed than the other one, though, in which case the unilingual utterances in the weaker language may resemble those of younger monolinguals.

Stories

In the course of the fourth year, BFLA children start to use complex sentences, which consist of a main clause and a subclause. This allows them to start connecting many ideas with each other and helps them to start telling short stories. Four-year-old BFLA children are getting quite good at telling stories, although there are huge differences between children in the complexity of their stories. When she was five, Marie told complicated French and English stories with ease, but Hiroko did not like to tell stories in either language.

Uneven Development

BFLA children's languages do not necessarily develop at the same pace. Children may know many more words in one language than the other, may produce complex sentences in one but not the other, and may tell stories in just a single language. When they are in the fifth year of life, BFLA children are acutely aware of their own abilities in each language. Kimmy knew that she was a great storyteller in English, and entertained people with her English stories, but she had trouble even forming complex sentences in Korean. This made her feel ashamed to speak Korean, and she became more and more reluctant to speak to her Korean grandparents—she wasn't able to express herself fluently in Korean, and she felt bad about that. She'd rather give up on speaking Korean. Her Korean grandparents, however, did not speak any English. Kimmy's mother felt deeply ashamed towards her parents that she had not managed to bring up a child who spoke their language.

Language Choice and Language Loss

Once BFLA children can say words in each language, they must select a language to use. This selection or choice takes place quite unconsciously, but already follows some rules. Typically, toddlers choose the language that their conversational partner speaks at the time of the conversation. At 17 months, Marie wasn't able to say sentences yet, but most of the time when she addressed her French-speaking mother, she spoke French, and when she addressed her English-speaking father, her words tended to be in English. Pedro did the same, depending on what language his parents happened to address him in. They spoke to him in Spanish when they were discussing food, and Pedro then also spoke Spanish; they spoke to him in English when they discussed his Superman toys, and Pedro followed suit. Thus, Pedro learned to do as his parents, that is, discuss different topics in different languages. Pedro also used some mixed utterances, with Spanish and English words. Because his parents both understood both languages and because many people in their environment also used mixed utterances, Pedro was just doing what seemed natural and fit in with what his family and friends. In contrast, Marie's parents did not like it when Marie used French and English words in a single sentence. They would stop and comment on it and ask her to repeat her sentence with just French or English words, depending on whom she was speaking to. Children thus get socialized into speaking mixed utterances, or just unilingual ones, very much like they are taught to say "please" and "thank you." At any rate, using mixed utterances is not a sign of cognitive or linguistic confusion.

Just before her second birthday, Hiroko tended to speak Japanese to her mother and English to her father. Afterwards she also started to speak English to her mother. At first Hiroko's mother didn't notice and just continued speaking Japanese to Hiroko, but after a while she got worried about Hiroko not speaking enough Japanese. She decided to ask a specialist and found out that it really matters how parents respond when BFLA children address them in the unexpected language (De Houwer, 2021). Instead of just continuing with the conversation when Hiroko spoke English to her, Hiroko's mother started to ask (in Japanese) "what?," "what did you mean?" and soon Hiroko started repeating her originally English utterance in Japanese. This is how Hiroko's mother managed to turn things around and get Hiroko to usually speak Japanese with her again, even when her father was present.

Kimmy's mother was not so lucky. Kimmy also started speaking English to her mother (instead of Korean) and Kimmy's mother did not know how to respond. She repeated in Korean what Kimmy had said in English but soon gave up because it made conversations very arduous and didn't seem to make Kimmy switch back to Korean. When Kimmy was alone with her mother, she often continued to speak Korean, though, so Kimmy's mother wasn't all too worried. However, as time went on and Kimmy's mother had less time to spend with Kimmy, these moments alone were few and far between, and Kimmy's Korean became much less developed than her English. Kimmy started not to want to speak Korean with anyone, including her Korean monolingual grandparents. This language loss greatly saddened the grandparents (and Kimmy's mother, who felt ashamed towards her parents that she had not managed to transmit their language to their granddaughter). Thus, Kimmy's relatives were not experiencing Harmonious Bilingualism.

External Threats to Harmonious Bilingualism

Threats to Harmonious Bilingualism within the family arise because BFLA children do not speak one of their languages at a more or less age-appropriate level. As the example from Kimmy shows, it is children themselves who may start rejecting one of their languages. Such rejection is the result of many factors. In Kimmy's case, Korean had always been the less frequently heard language, giving Kimmy fewer opportunities to practice speaking it herself. It did not help that Kimmy's father basically took no interest in Korean. Also at her English-speaking child care center and later preschool, Korean received no attention whatsoever. It was as if the Korean part of Kimmy's life did not exist. These experiences both at home and at school must have given Kimmy the impression that Korean was far less valued and far less socially important than English.

In contrast, Pedro had heard lots of both Spanish and English. When he started to attend preschool, the teachers there mostly used English, but they knew a bit of Spanish and regularly asked him to teach them a few more Spanish words. They even had maps of the world in the classroom showing where people spoke Spanish (and English). This made Pedro proud of both his languages and kept him from developing negative attitudes towards Spanish. By age five he told goofy stories in both languages that made everybody laugh. Hiroko, however, never got to that point. By age five, she was attending a Japanese-speaking preschool and still speaking English at home with her father. However, as I wrote earlier, she did not like to tell stories. She was rather shy and did not engage much with her peers at school or speak much. Her teacher was worried and told Hiroko's mother that it would be best to stop using English at home, because, surely, English was keeping Hiroko from fully developing her Japanese. Hiroko's parents were shocked when they heard this, but they wanted first and foremost for Hiroko to do well at school and were willing to do anything to help her. They believed the teacher and Hiroko's father did his best to speak Japanese to Hiroko instead of English. Since Hiroko was born, he had made a bit of progress in Japanese but because he worked at home and wrote in English for work, he did not have many opportunities to learn Japanese. Hiroko would not accept her father speaking "bad" Japanese to her and did not understand why he no longer spoke English. It was a very frustrating and painful time. Rather than develop her Japanese, Hiroko became depressed and was no longer speaking much at home (let alone at school). Her mother decided to consult the expert again who had earlier helped her to get Hiroko to speak Japanese to her. The expert explained that taking away one language never helps the other language, and that English was fundamental because it was the language Hiroko used to communicate with her father. Furthermore, according to the United Nations Child Rights Convention (www. unicef.org/child-rights-convention/convention-text), educational institutions should foster respect for all the languages children bring to school.

Although Marie spoke French and English very well, several of her relatives expressed concerns about her bilingualism, saying that it was bad for her. Marie's parents felt very upset and sometimes insecure when they heard this and did not know how to respond. Einar's mother was upset to hear her son's pediatrician advise her to give up on speaking Norwegian to Einar. The pediatrician claimed that hearing Norwegian on top of German would slow down Einar's overall development.

Table 7.1 Important developmental milestones

TIMING (Roughly)	LANGUAGE ELEMENTS
Between 0.6 and 1	Babbling in repeated syllables
By age 1	Understanding words in each of two languages
Soon after age 1	Understanding some words in each language with similar meanings Saying what appear to be single words
Between 1.6 and age 2	Noticeable increase in the number of different words said Saying words in each language
Around age 2	Saying two words in one breath
Between 2.6 and age 3	Saying short sentences with three or four words in the right order in at least one language
Around age 3.6	Being mostly understandable to unfamiliar adults who speak the same language(s)
Around age 4	Saying sentences consisting of a main clause and a subclause, in at least one language
Between 4.6 and age 5	Ability to tell a short story that hangs together, in at least one language

Unfortunately, such negative attitudes towards early bilingualism are present all over the Western world. While they negatively affect families' senses of well-being, the good news is that early bilingualism, like early monolingualism, does not harm children in any way. The important milestones for early language development are the same (Table 7.1), regardless of whether children grow up with two languages or just one from birth (De Houwer, 2021; Sundara, 2022).

Conclusion

Children who hear two languages in the home from birth can learn to use these languages fluently and proficiently. Like children learning just a single language, they need a lot of supportive language input. Differences among families in how much and in which circumstances they use each language can explain much of the wide, normal variability among bilingual children. It is important that bilingual children experience a communicative need to actually speak each language. Unfortunately, negative attitudes towards early bilingualism and ignoring one of children's languages may work against Harmonious Bilingual Development. Advocacy and information resources based on the latest research (e.g. see www.habilnet.org) can help overcome these hurdles.

Closing Reflections

1   How might you draw on the research knowledge in this chapter to implement new theory-to-practice connections in your work with multilingual children and families?
2   Consider Kimmy and the meta-messages she received that contributed to her rejection of Korean. How can practitioners foster positive language learning environments for languages/cultures in which they are not conversant, fluent, or knowledgeable?

References

De Houwer, A. (2006). Le développement harmonieux ou non harmonieux du bilinguisme de l'enfant au sein de la famille. *Langage et Société*, 116(2), 29–49. doi:10.3917/ls.116.0029.
De Houwer, A. (2009). *Bilingual first language acquisition*. Multilingual Matters.
De Houwer, A. (2020). Harmonious bilingualism: Well-being for families in bilingual settings. In S. Eisenchlas & A. Schalley (Eds.), *Handbook of home language maintenance and development* (pp. 63–83). Mouton de Gruyter.
De Houwer, A. (2021). *Bilingual development in childhood*. Cambridge University Press. doi:10.1017/9781108866002.
Genesee, F., Paradis, J., & Crago, M. B. (2004). *Dual language development & disorders: A handbook on bilingualism & second language learning*. Paul H. Brookes Publishing.
Head Zauche, L., Darcy Mahoney, A., Thul, T., Zauche, M., Weldon, A., & Stapel-Wax, J. (2017). The power of language nutrition for children's brain development, health, and future academic achievement. *Journal of Pediatric Health Care*, 31(4), 493–503. doi:10.1016/j.pedhc.2017.01.007.
Hollebeke, I., Struys, E., & Agirdag, O. (2020). Can family language policy predict linguistic, socioemotional and cognitive child and family outcomes? A systematic review. *Journal of Multilingual and Multicultural Development* [online ahead of print]. doi:10.1080/01434632.2020.1858302.

Müller, L-M., Howard, K., Wilson, E., Gibson, J., & Katsos, N. (2020). Bilingualism in the family and child well-being: A scoping review. *International Journal of Bilingualism*, 24(5–6). doi:10.1177/1367006920920939.

Sundara, M. (2022). Development of speech perception and production in bilingual preverbal infants. In B. Goldstein (Ed.), *Bilingual language development and disorders in Spanish- English speakers* (3rd ed.) (pp. 67–94). Brookes Publishing.

Wölck, W. (1987/1988). Types of natural bilingual behavior: A review and revision. *The Bilingual Review/La Revista Bilingüe*, 14, 3–16.

8 Supporting Infants and Toddlers in Bilingual Classrooms

Azul Muller

Opening Reflections

1   If you work in a bilingual setting with infants and toddlers, what areas of your teaching and interactions with young children would you like to strengthen?
2   What do you see as critical elements for connecting bilingualism, play, and social interaction in infant and toddler settings?

Introduction

In this chapter, I describe ideas and strategies for supporting infants and toddlers and their families in classrooms following a bilingual/multilingual model for language learning. I also share my personal multilingual journey and my professional journey as a teacher and mentor supporting children's multilingual needs and talents in my infant and toddler classroom. Last, I discuss how Learning Stories and other assessment measures can document children's and families' multilingual learning and growth.

My Multilingual Journey

Within my family, there are two different cultures: Mexican and American. I speak, read, and write in two languages, with English as my first, primary language. As a young girl growing up in Orange County, California, I found myself stuck between the two cultures, and my school community did not reflect my multicultural and multilingual identity. Although I learned Spanish within my family, it wasn't encouraged at school. As I continued to learn my family's language history, I wanted to explore my Chicana identity, and I relied on my mother and my childhood caretakers as I experienced bilingual first language acquisition (BFLA) with two first languages, Language A and Language Alpha. My family often said, "You will have so many more opportunities because you know English and Spanish," and their wisdom guides my work as a bilingual infant and toddler teacher and mentor.

Context of my Work

My school, the Family Developmental Center, is part of Felton Institute's Children, Youth, and Families Division, Early Childhood Education Programs. Located in the Mission district of San Francisco, our school reflects the neighborhood's first and second-generation immigrant families from Mexico and Central America. The school consists of

DOI: 10.4324/9781003227816-12

two infant classrooms, four toddler classrooms, and four preschool classrooms. Thirty percent of the children across our sites have additional needs and/or disabilities. Our Title V program emphasizes a play-based emergent curriculum, a language philosophy that embraces multilingual families, and wrap-around service programs. Our bilingual model supports children's native language (Spanish) and the learning of English. Five of the ten classrooms are designated as dual- language classrooms, where one teacher only speaks one language (the teacher's native language) and all teachers speak English.

The Classroom Context

Our school philosophy links emergent curriculum (Jones & Nimmo, 1994) with teacher inquiry (Castle, 2012; Kroll & Meier, 2017) to identify children's interests and implement an intentional language, play, and social curriculum. Our inquiry cycle involves observing, reflecting, planning, observing again, and documenting children's learning. The children in our infant and toddler settings explore big concepts of autonomy, trust, exploration, attachment, and identity within the classroom. My infant and toddler classroom consists of twelve children ranging in age from 5–9 months, and by year's end our eldest child is 20 months old. We use PITC's primary care model approach (see Chapters 2 and 3) to ensure that all children's primary needs and supports are provided by a consistent teacher. As a bilingual classroom we utilize the school's philosophy of the teacher-based model for language modeling. For instance, in my classroom, 90 percent of the children come from monolingual Spanish homes with the other 10 percent from Spanish/ English bilingual homes. We use a family questionnaire to learn about families' language experiences and goals, information that we use to plan our bilingual curriculum.

Routines and the Environment Promote Multilingualism

Relationships as embedded in classroom routines and an engaging physical environment are at the center of my school's approach and my personal philosophy of bilingual education.

Routines, Environments, and Materials

Caregiving and relationship-building are the foundation of our curriculum, and intimate moments at meal times, diaper changing, book sharing, and physical exploration all promote bilingualism through social relationships. Within the routines, we emphasize turn-taking, repetition, facial expressions, gestures, and symbols to foster language acquisition. Through guided participation, we foster children's capabilities to understand, speak and participate during routines and social relationships, and empower children to grow as individuals and community members. We also use scaffolding techniques and child-directed speech to narrate the process of each step of a routine so children feel successful and included socially.

For example, the narration and communication exchange during a diaper routine allows children to participate actively and engage in one-on-one interactions with caregivers. I acknowledge children's responses during diapering routines by responding to their babbling or words to let them know that I am listening and value their speech. I also extend their verbalizations by narrating the routine and pause to allow children to verbally and nonverbally contribute to our communicative exchange, which encourages children's problem-solving and social connections (Bedrova & Leong, 2018).

We also expand children's bilingualism through engagement with indoor and outdoor environments and materials that encourage hands-on creativity and exploration (Wanerman,

2013). We plan our routines, activities, and provocations to encourage collaborative language exploration of the physical environments and materials—"children can perform much more skillfully together with others than" alone (de Haan & Singer, 2003, p. 7). For instance, with small objects that infants manipulate and put into their mouths, we narrate their playful exploration to extend bilingual vocabulary and language. For both infants and toddlers, we promote children's independent physical exploration of our bilingual books, and communal interactions as I read each book in Spanish first and then my co-teacher, who models English, reads in English. We use mostly bilingual books and some books in either Spanish or English; once children are familiar with a book in one language, we read and talk about that book in the other language on another day. In addition, we each lead a large group music and book time in either Spanish or English, which allows children to sing and move in varied indoor and outdoor spaces.

Culturally Responsive Communication with Families

My colleagues and I intentionally design structures and strategies to communicate and dialogue with our families about the challenges and benefits of bilingual education. We utilize classroom visits, a family language questionnaire, informal daily conversations, Learning Stories, and twice-a-year parent conferences.

Visiting the School and Classroom

After the enrollment process, new parents are invited to spend a few hours on each of the first two days of school with their infants. The children then attend for half days before integrating to our full day program after one week. We also honor the families' languages by inviting them to interact with their children in the classroom, and we engage in informal open conversations. For example, I documented in my teaching journal eight-month-old Angel's first day at school as he gained safety and support from his mother:

> August 16, 2018—Angel's first day
> I open the door for Ana, mother of 8-month-old Angel, on his first day at the center. She is welcomed in, and she turns to Angel to whisper, "*Esta es tu maestra*" (This is your teacher). As Ana settles into the classroom and puts on her shoe covers, she nervously smiles and makes her way to the carpet area, and sets Angel down beside her and begins to introduce herself and her son to the classroom. Not surprisingly, Angel stays close to mom for comfort. As we talk about our classroom routines compared with their home routines, I learn that Angel has begun crawling and exploring his home environment. During this interaction, I am curious to see how Angel adjusts to our classroom and I am excited to begin my interactions with him. He looks for mom's approval, and she says, "*Estas bien, mira el patito,*" (You are okay, look at the ducky) and nods her head with a smile, and offers a duck toy nearby to encourage exploration of the new space. After this reassurance, Angel begins to crawl toward the different materials, looking back at mom to see if she is still there. Mom explains to me, "*Puede ser tímido en lugares nuevos*" (He can be shy in new places).

Our intentional use of bilingual communication in the classrooms with families sends the message that their languages are valued and honored in our educational space.

Family Communication and Partnership

Our open dialogue about multilingual goals and strategies continues daily in informal conversations with families, and through twice-a-year parent conferences. We also invite families to participate in any classroom routines when they bring their children to school in the morning. The typical morning routine begins with offering breakfast for the children and joining morning free play. During morning routines, teachers and families talk about the children's morning so far, do family check-ins, and share stories of children's learning at home and at school. Many young infants begin to transition to solid foods during their time in the classroom, and talking with families during the morning routine allows us to learn new information about children's development around feeding. We also learn about children's favorite foods, possible allergies, and even their developmental capacity to eat from a spoon. We also invite families to share favorite bilingual songs and stories from home to encourage bilingual home-school connections. Our family friendly morning routines, then, allow for authentic bilingual conversations focusing on families' bilingual talents, interests, and needs (Table 8.1).

The consistent use of bilingual communication encourages families to trust us and to engage in conversation that deepens over the course of our time together.

Table 8.1 Morning routines and possible conversations

Morning Routine	Possible Topics	Possible Questions
Breakfast	• Feeding routines • Family experiences • Child's development	• How does ___ like to eat their oat cereal? • What foods have you tried at home? • Are there any allergies you have noticed? • Is your child able to swallow their food from the spoon? • Cómo le gusta comer su hijo/a el cereal de avena? • ¿Qué alimentos ha probado en casa? • ¿Hay alguna alergia que haya notado? • ¿Su hijo/a puede usar la cuchara para comer?
Free Play	• Family experiences • Child's learning at home • Child's interests • New language or motor movements seen • Family culture/histories • Sleeping habits • Classroom experiences	• What is the home routine like? • Who are the people in ___'s life? • Tell me more about ___? • How is language part of the home routine? • I'm curious, how is ___ (walking/crawling/vocalizations/engagement) at home? • ¿Cómo es la rutina del hogar? • ¿Quiénes son las personas en la vida de ___? • ¿Cuéntame más sobre ___? • ¿Cómo es el lenguaje parte de la rutina del hogar? • Tengo curiosidad, ¿cómo está ___ (caminando / gateando / vocalizando / involucrando) en casa?

Bilingualism and Assessments

As teachers in a Title V early childhood education center, we use both mandated and non-mandated assessments to provide ongoing classroom observations and documentation of children's language development and learning in other domains.

Desired Results Developmental Profile

We use the mandated Desired Results Developmental Profile (DRDP) (2015) infant and toddler assessment tool to document children's development and progress. The DRDP (2015) infant and toddler tool consists of five of the eight domains in the DRDP (2015) version for older children: (1) approaches to learning–self-regulation; (2) social and emotional development; (3) language and literacy development; (4) cognition: including math and science; and (5) physical development–health. We use the DRDP for a more authentic and meaningful portrait of children's learning in their primary language.

Learning Stories

We have also recently selected Learning Stories as a non-mandated form of documentation to complement the DRDP. Learning Stories are a form of authentic assessment from New Zealand (Carr & Lee, 2012) that document key moments in children's learning and growth, and are stories written directly to children. While most Learning Stories are written to and about one child, they can focus on a small group of children. The Te Whāriki framework emphasizes critical pedagogy and a commitment to the "notion that the Maori language and culture are to be protected" (Lee et al., 2013, p. 35), and is a bicultural document "where theory, culture, and practice were interwoven, rooted in *te ao Māori—*the Māori world" (Escamilla, 2021). Learning Stories also capture children's learning dispositions, which are "habits of mind, tendencies to respond to situations in certain ways" (Carr, 2001, p. 21). Learning Stories also focus on what children "can do" rather than what "they cannot" (Hatherly & Sands, 2002, p. 11), and chronicle key developmental plot points in children's bilingual development (Escamilla et al., 2021).

The Learning Stories that I write for my children follow the most prevalent Learning Stories structure from New Zealand (Carr & Lee, 2012):

> *What is happening?* Describe what a child does and says from a subjective teacher perspective.
> *What does it mean?* Describe the pedagogical value of what the child said and/or did, still with a subjective perspective.
> *Opportunities and possibilities:* Describe ideas and strategies for extending the child's learning.
> *Family comments:* Invite families to respond to the story or ask specific questions to the family to extend the conversation.

Basic Elements of a Learning Story

- What is happening?
- What does it mean?
- Opportunities and possibilities
- Family comments

In many of the Learning Stories, I also include relevant bilingual goals from our school and specific DRDP measures that I feel capture elements of the particular child's learning. I find that Learning Stories effectively help bilingual families to recognize and celebrate important milestones in their children's bilingual learning, as well as offering families a rare opportunity to contribute their own feelings and thoughts about their children's learning and growth.

Alexa's Learning Story—"Book Magic"

Early in the year, eleven-month-old Alexa showed a keen interest in exploring books on her own, with adults, and invited others to "read" with her. I documented Alexa's book handling behaviors (Schickendanz, 1999) by a writing a Learning Story about Alexa's fondness for books and interest in looking at and engaging with books on her own and with adults. I wanted the Learning Story to capture the power of her developing interest in books and to show Alexa and her family the value of books for making bilingual connections to print. The Learning Story is based on one afternoon when Alexa brought a book to a pillow in the soft area and invited a peer to "read" with her. Alexa looked at the book as she held it up upside down, and I did not turn the book right-side up because I did not want to deter her exploration and engagement with the book. I originally wrote the Learning Story in Spanish to honor Alexa's and her family's Spanish home language, and Alexa's mother responded to the Learning Story with a written note in Spanish. I include the entire Learning Story here, with the original first section in Spanish.

LIBRO DE MAGIA—BOOK MAGIC

¿Qué Sucedió?   Alexa, esta tarde, cuando terminamos tu bocadillo, viniste al área de peluches, miraste alrededor del aula y recogiste un libro que estaba en el estante cercano. Fue un libro que leímos durante el día durante nuestra música matutina y el tiempo de lectura. Cogiste el libro y lo llevaste a la almohada en el suelo. Soltaste el libro mientras acomodabas la almohada, te inclinaste hacia atrás y levantaste la pierna hasta la rodilla. Te mirabas tan cómoda. Una vez que te acomodaste, levantaste el libro por las rodillas para estabilizarlo y comenzaste a abrir las páginas. Empezaste a vocalizar algunos sonidos y te pregunté: "¿Estás leyendo Alexa?" miraste a un lado del libro y respondiste con más vocalizaciones. Además de vocalizar tu respuesta, tocaste el lugar junto a ti y volviste a leer tu libro. En ese momento me pregunté si me invitabas a unirme a ti. Mantuve mi distancia para seguir observando tu próximo momento de aprendizaje. Gael estaba sentado a mi lado y te miró mientras yo te hacía la pregunta. Supongo que entendió tu movimiento y se sentó junto a ti, mirando lo que estabas haciendo. Miró hacia arriba y vocalizó y señaló las imágenes en el libro, Gael en respuesta se inclinó más cerca de la almohada y vocalizó en respuesta. Ambos miraron algunas páginas juntos, terminaron el libro y lo volvieron a colocar en el estante cercano. Maestra Azul

What Happened?   Alexa, this afternoon when we had finished your snack, you came over to the soft toy area, you looked around the room and gathered a book that was on the nearby shelf. It was a book we read during the day during our morning music and book time. You picked up the book and brought it with you to the pillow on the floor. You set the book down as you got comfortable on the pillow, leaning back and crossing your leg over the other. You seemed so comfortable. Once you got settled, you brought the book up by your knees to stabilize it and began to open the pages. You began to vocalize some sounds and I asked, "Are you reading, Alexa?" You looked to the side of the book and responded with more vocalizations. Along with vocalizing your response, you patted to the spot right next to you and went back to reading your book. At that moment I wondered if you patted the floor for me to join you. I kept my distance to continue observing your next learning moment. Gael had been sitting right next to me and looked at you while I asked you the question. I assume he understood your cue and he joined you, sitting near you and looking at what you were doing. You looked up and vocalized and pointed to the pictures in the book. Gael in response leaned closer over the pillow and vocalized in response. You both looked at a few pages together, finished the book, and put it back on the nearby shelf.

What Does This Mean?   Alexa your invitation today with your book reading showed me something new, as I revisit the moment, I assume you patted the floor for myself or Gael to join you in your reading. I wonder if this is something you may be imitating from the teachers in the classroom. I have noticed that you have built a bond with Teacher Blanca, and when she calls you over, she waves her hand in a come here motion and pats the spot next to her, and you go over to give her a hug. I also noticed your vocalizations and your attention to the photos in the books. Your interest in literacy has grown so much. While you were pointing, smiling, and vocalizing at the different pages, you were being so expressive to communicate your interest in the book.

Opportunities and Possibilities   As I think about your mother's response [below] and my own wonders about the development of your early reading stages, I want to continue to explore your love for books. I plan on placing books in more than just our library area so that you can access them in different spaces. I would also like to join you next time and ask you questions about the pictures you are noticing. I plan to extend your language by using parallel and self-talk while reading the book with you.

Related DRDP Measures

- Imitation
- Curiosity and Initiative in Learning
- Relationships and Social Interactions with Peers
- Responsiveness to Language
- Communication and Use of Language (Expressive)
- Interest in Literacy

Family Comment   Alexa is so funny; she brings me and my husband so much joy with the little things she does. I am happy to see that Alexa is sharing because she doesn't like to share with her older sister. I think it is beautiful that you have been able to capture many stories of Alexa's love for books. At home we don't have a big collection of books but here she is able to access them. Alexa has learned so much in your classroom and I am happy to see her trying to talk. She does the same thing at home, yet I can't make out her words yet, but it's a good thing her sister helps me a little bit.

This Learning Story helped preserve a moment in developmental time of Alexa's early love for books, and her mother's response in Spanish also validates their home language. In these ways, the Learning Story serves as a cultural and language bridge between school and home for Alexa and her family.

Figure 8.1 Alexa reading a book

Figure 8.2 Alexa and Gael engaging in book reading

Final Thoughts

I strongly believe that the daily practices of observing children, building relationships, honoring children's identities, and use of effective bilingual assessments support each child and promote a strong bilingual community. Our ultimate goal, though, is to go beyond honoring families' languages and cultures, and instead to cultivate a meaningful and engaging bilingual curriculum for academic success and social inclusion during the infant and toddler years and beyond. As I continue to work with young children and their families, I will continue to strive for sustainable practices that support the bilingual program model and ensure that children feel that their languages and cultures are valued.

Closing Reflections

1   What are the benefits of the bilingual model and strategies that Azul and her colleagues use?
2   How might you adapt and use Learning Stories as an authentic form of bilingual assessment for children and families?

References

Bodrova, E., & Leong, D. J. (2018). Tools of the mind: A Vygotskian early childhood curriculum. In M. Fleer & B. van Oers (Eds.), *International handbook of early childhood education* (pp. 1095–1111). Springer.

Carr, M. (2001). *Assessment in early childhood settings: Learning stories*. Sage.

Carr, M., & Lee, W. (2012). *Learning stories: Constructing learner identities in early education*. Sage.

Castle, K. (2012). *Early childhood teacher research: From questions to results*. Routledge.

Escamilla, I. M., Kroll, L., Meier, D., & White, A. (2021). *Learning stories and teacher inquiry groups: Reimagining teaching and assessment in early childhood education*. National Association for the Education of Young Children.

Escamilla, I. M. (2021). Learning stories—Improving dual-language instruction, assessment, and teacher inquiry in preschool education. Doctoral dissertation, San Francisco State University.

de Haan, D., & Singer, E. (2003). 'Use your words' A sociocultural approach to the teacher's role in the transition from physical to verbal strategies of resolving Peer conflicts among toddlers. *Journal of Early Childhood Research*, 1(1), 95–109.

Hatherly, A., & Sands, L. (2002). So what is different about learning stories. *The First Years: Nga Tau Tuatahi. New Zealand Journal of Infant and Toddler Education*, 4(1), 8–12. Retrieved from https://elp.co.nz/wp-content/uploads/2021/03/So-What-is-different-about-Learning-Stories.pdf.

Jones, E., & Nimmo, J. (1994). *Emergent curriculum*. National Association for the Education of Young Children.

Kroll, L. K., & Meier, D. R. (Eds.). (2017). *Documentation and inquiry in the early childhood classroom: Research stories of engaged practitioners in urban centers and schools*. Routledge.

Lee, W., Carr, M., Soutar, B., & Mitchell, L. (2013). *Understanding the Te Whariki approach: Early years education in practice*. Routledge.

Schickendanz, J. A. (1999). *Much more than the ABCs: The early stages of reading and writing*. National Association for the Education of Young Children.

Wanerman, T. (2013). *From handprints to hypotheses: Using the project approach with toddlers and twos*. Redleaf Press.

9 Supporting Multilingualism for Infants and Toddlers in English-Medium Classrooms

Seferina Rivera

Opening Reflections

1   What is your current knowledge about supporting infants and toddlers' multi-lingualism in an English-medium setting?
2   If you are not conversant in all of the children's languages in your setting, what strategies do you use to support multilingual children's languages, play, and interaction?

Introduction

As a second-generation Chicana on my father's side and second-generation Russian Jew on my mother's side, my family experienced generational language loss. My grandparents lived in the United States when assimilation into the dominant American culture was a priority for success and survival, which happened at the cost of not passing on Spanish and Yiddish and our linguistic-cultural identity. So much progressive educational peda-gogy, though, recognizes the benefits of multilingualism for children's overall well-being (De Houwer, 2009; Weise & Serna, 2021). While I cannot communicate with all my classroom's children and families fluently in their home languages, I find ways to support children's multilingualism and expose the monolingual, English-speaking children to other languages. In this chapter, I describe my multilingual teaching philosophy within my classroom and school context, and I highlight three main elements of multilingual language support: gathering information from families, interactional strategies, and incorporating home-school connections into the curriculum.

My Teaching Context

I have taught infants and toddlers for 31 years. For the last 20 years I have been a head infant-toddler teacher at Mills College Children's School, and work with paid teaching assistants and Mills College student teachers. The classroom consists of 12 children, who range from 5 months to 26 months at the beginning of the school year, and by year's end our oldest children are around 3 years old. My multilingual teaching philosophy emphasizes understanding families' cultural and linguistic identities and integrating those identities in the classroom.

My classroom uses the primary caregiving model (see Chapters 2, 3, and 8), and the children are assigned primary teachers who greet the children and families on arrival, carry out diapering, napping, and feeding routines, and provide emotional support. Each

DOI: 10.4324/9781003227816-13

teacher is assigned 2–3 primary children. If there is a student teacher who speaks a child's home language, we match them in a caregiving group and the teacher uses their shared home language and English. Because my colleagues and I participate in all classroom routines and activities, all children are exposed to more than one language, which encourages children to listen to and respect multiple languages.

While my classroom is primarily monolingual English-speaking, the children's family languages have included Spanish, Thai, Korean, Russian, Mandarin, Cantonese, Hebrew, Tagalog, Portuguese, Hindi, Farsi, Japanese, Kannada, and French. Some children enter school with no English experience, while others experience English and another home language with their families. There are also many parents who no longer feel fluent in their home language, even though they include some home language vocabulary mixed with English at home.

In my mixed-age classroom, I also practice play-based emergent curriculum (Jones & Nimmo, 1994), and provide materials and experiences responsive to children's growing competencies and interests in each other (Figure 9.1).

Families engage with their children on a daily basis in my classroom, and I document these multilingual family interactions to inform my curriculum (Figure 9.2). These interactions also showcase family and cultural preferences for interaction and play, which deepen home-school connections around language, play, and interaction.

Strategies for Supporting Multilingual Children and Families

In describing our approach and strategies to promote social and multilingual learning, I provide examples from Artemis, Consuelo, and Nyima, and their families. Artemis was 7 months old at the start of the school year. Her father speaks to her in Spanish and English and Artemis's mother mostly speaks English with her. Artemis's grandparents, an integral part of her life, speak to her in English, Japanese, and Chinese. In addition, her parents are teaching her sign language. Consuelo started school just before her first birthday. Her parents speak to her in Spanish and English. She has two older bilingual siblings who mostly speak in English at home but respond confidently to either language.

Figure 9.1 Nyima and Artemis at play

Figure 9.2 Artemis and her father interact

Nyima began school at 20 months old. Her primary language at home is French with some Tibetan included. Her four-year old brother, who attends a different English-speaking classroom at our school, uses some English at home with their parents but mostly speaks French. Our school is Nyima's first direct exposure to English.

Gathering Information from Families

Families are the most important resource for caregiving and curriculum development and meeting the needs of multilingual children (Weise & Serna, 2021). For collecting information and guiding our early conversations, I rely on the Infant Needs and Service Plan, a form required by California State Licensing for children under two (California Department of Social Services, 2020, §§101419.2 and 101419.3). It must be updated by parents every 3 months, and asks about children's eating, sleeping, and diapering/toileting routines as well as family life. It provides an effective structure for establishing that parents are the experts in caring for their children. When working with multilingual children, I am especially interested in finding out the names for family members, key words for comfort and safety that families want us to use, and special words for sleeping and diapering. I also pay close attention to the developmental multilingual milestones that parents share for their younger and older toddlers. I use all of this information to observe and recognize children's nonverbal communication attempts and early words, document children's play interests and preferences, and use this knowledge to set up and monitor my classroom environment.

Home Visits

Before a child begins their first day at school, the family is offered a home visit. The lead teacher (who guides the classroom when I am not present), and I meet with the child, parents, and occasionally other family members living in the home. I use the Infant Needs and Service Plan form as a guide for the conversation while the lead teacher records detailed notes. Sharing this information in a family's home starts a dialogue of trust and communication with families around their cultural, linguistic, and educational goals, values, and practices.

For instance, during a visit to Nyima's home, I listened intently while Nyima's mom described the diaper changing process. My lead teacher, Cayley, carefully wrote down the description. Nyima (20 months) played with a train set on the floor between us and watched her mom, who described the diapering experience to me in English. Nyima asked her mom in French what she was saying. Mom told her in French that her new teacher is learning about how she gets her "diaper" changed. Then she told me, "She doesn't know the word 'diaper.' We call it *couche*. We tell her, '*change la couche*'." Cayley phonetically spelled "*change la couche*" on the form. I repeated the phrase and asked for confirmation that I said it correctly. I let mom know that we would learn this phrase, teach it to all of the other teachers, and use it when it is time for diapering.

When I visited Artemis and her family in their home, Artemis (6 months) lay on her tummy and reached for a toy just beyond her reach. "You are almost there *mi amor*," her father, Rudy, told her. When she started to grimace, Rudy told her, "*No te preocupes* [Don't worry]. I can help." He brought the toy closer and she grasped it. "So how do you refer to yourselves to Artemis?" I asked. "I am Daddy and Elise is Mama," Rudy told me while he and Artemis gazed into each other's eyes and smiled.

"My parents come to visit us any chance they get," Elise told me. "They are a really important part of her life." "How wonderful to have their support. How do you refer to them for Artemis?" I asked. "My dad is called *Gung Gung*. My mom is called *Obachan*." Artemis looked up at her mom when she heard these names. "We are talking about your *Gung Gung* and your *Obachan*," Elise told Artemis. "She really knows their names," I commented. "I am asking all of our families to create a family page that I will put into a book for the children to look at. Whomever you consider family you can include on your page and write in the names for all of the people so that we can talk to Artemis about them." Rudy looked at me and smiled, "That will be really wonderful."

During these home visits I learn important information about parent-child communication and culturally influenced language use that can only be gathered through observation. I also use these visits to create a chart of the children's names to use in the classroom, which ensures that we use their correct names when we sing and talk about who is picking them up. The home visits also help us see first-hand how family members provide responsive and respectful language interactions with their children. For example, Nyima's question about the conversation demonstrated her trusting relationship with her mother and strong communication skills for a 20-month-old. The parents wanted Nyima to be immersed in French, and to have this strong base before being introduced to English. They planned to continue only to speak French with some Tibetan spoken by mom in their home. Her mother was open to the idea of using key vocabulary in French to build bridges to her new school setting.

I also noticed how Artemis's father bathed Artemis in supportive language, moving fluidly between English and Spanish. Artemis was afforded a lot of verbal input linked to what she was experiencing, she was included in the conversation, and she seemed to recognize familiar names. Her parents were delighted that Artemis could be matched with a Spanish-speaking primary teacher and there would also be a Japanese-speaking student teacher present. They hoped that she would develop an ability to understand and communicate to some degree in her four home languages as well as sign language.

Parent Teacher Conferences

Our new children start school in August, and then three months later we update the Needs and Service Plan form when I meet with parents for a conference. During this time,

I share with families our Learning Stories and photo documentation that highlight the children's experiences and developmental progression at school. We also revisit any changes that have occurred from the parents' perspective on the Needs and Service Plan Form. For multilingual children in particular, we layer children's language development at school with parents' home observations to capture the full picture of their competencies (WIDA, 2015). Keeping track of the growth of children's dual language skills is important for considering how both home and school can contribute to Harmonious Bilingualism.

We also revisit a family's home language information beyond the initial home visit. As my relationships with families evolve and we develop more trust, families sometimes feel more comfortable sharing new aspects of their multilingual goals and practices. I have also observed three main reasons that families might hesitate to share their multilingualism early in the school year:

- they consider it a burden to ask teachers to learn words in their language;
- they do not feel fully bilingual, so they didn't initially share all of the languages spoken in the home; and
- their home language is an intimate and private communication only spoken in the family, though families are often open to changing their minds later.

As our relationships deepen over time, I do offer recommendations and information about the importance of children retaining their languages at home and school.

Supporting Multilingualism Through Caregiving and Interactional Strategies

Since I teach in a mixed-age classroom, I support children's language and communication specific to each child's development. Many of the strategies that work for a young infant work across the age span, but I also add new strategies as children's languages and cognition evolve and their interests expand. I am also mindful that "the core of effective interactional strategies in working with multilingual infants and toddlers is attuned and reciprocal exchanges with an emphasis on non-verbal aspects of communication" (Weise & Serna, 2021).

Artemis and Diaper Changing

Artemis lays on the diaper changing table while Yui, my student teacher, asks in English, "Do you want to hold your diaper?" as she holds the diaper within Artemis' reach and waits for Artemis to respond. Artemis takes the diaper and shakes it up and down while repeating the sound "Aaa. Aaaa. Aaa." "Aaaa, aaaa, aaa," Yui says, "I like your sounds, Artemis." Artemis watches Yui's face as she speaks and then repeats her sounds and shaking movements. When Artemis pauses, Yui continues, "That's your special diaper that Mama and Dada brought for you from your home. I am going to take your wet diaper off and put that fresh one on." Artemis continues to watch Yui, who speaks Japanese and now sings a playful song in Japanese as she changes her diaper. Yui remembers that Artemis' grandmother speaks Japanese and wonders if she has heard this song before. Yui's face becomes animated and Artemis responds with wide eyes and a smile.

In this scene, although Artemis is not yet speaking and producing words in either English or Japanese, Yui utilizes both languages to engage with Artemis as mutual partners in their conversation and interaction. Artemis speaks to her by repeating the "aaa" pattern, and Yui responds with a comment in English as if Artemis understands. Yui also uses narration in English to engage with Artemis, as well as singing in Japanese to deepen their social and multilingual connection.

Consuelo and Her Book

Consuelo reaches into the book basket and finds one of her favorite books, *Brown Bear Brown Bear* (Martin & Carle, 1992). Consuelo takes the book out, hands it to her caregiver, Theresa, who sits nearby on the floor, and then sits next to her.

Theresa opens the book. Consuelo points to the picture of the bear. "Oh," Theresa, who speaks some Spanish, says. "*Es un oso* [It's a bear]." Consuelo looks up at Theresa and smiles. Before Theresa reads, Consuelo turns the page and points to the red bird. "*Si, es un pajaro rojo* [Yes, it's a red bird]," Theresa says. "*Pajo*," Consuelo replies. Again, Consuelo turns the page and points to the next animal, and Theresa continues naming each animal in Spanish to the end of book. Then Consuelo puts it in the book basket. She reaches for another book with animals on the cover, hands it to Theresa, and sits down next to her. In this book-sharing scene, Consuelo speaks a few Spanish words and primarily uses gestures, pointing, intonation, and some signs to communicate with the teacher (Figure 9.3).

Counselo has learned that Theresa will respond to her initiations for engagement and interaction and knows that her interests matter to Theresa. Counselo sets the pace for the interaction, and Theresa extends and expands on her ideas by adding more information and vocabulary in Spanish such as the animal names and colors to describe what Consuelo points at in the book.

Figure 9.3 Example of a teacher and 14-month-old Consuelo reading a book together using joint attention

Nyima at Play

> Nyima arrives at school one day with her mother and older brother Samten. They become interested in the dramatic play area, each finding their own baby to wrap in a blanket and hold. They speak to one another in French as they play. I stay close by and comment in English on what they are doing. After about 10 minutes of playing, her mom announces that it is time to say goodbye. Mom and Samten give Nyima a kiss and walk out the door. Nyima returns to playing. She carefully puts the baby in the highchair and then places the painted wooden watermelon to the baby's lips. I sit nearby on the floor, observing her actions and language. Nyima talks to herself throughout her play. I don't recognize her words. She turns to me and hands me a wooden carrot. "Thank you Nyima. *Merci.* You gave me a carrot. Should I feed the baby too?" I ask, as I hold the carrot to the baby, look at Nyima, and wait for a response. Nyima nods and says, "*Oui.*" In between participating in play with Nyima, I also take photographs and write notes to share later with Nyima and her family about her language and play.

In this scene, in addition to observing Nyima's nonverbal communication with me and the doll, I coordinate my oral language with body language, intonation, and pauses to highlight and extend my social interaction, play, and linguistic intentions. I am actively involved in her play, though careful not to distract or derail Nyima's intentions. Later, the photographs that I share with Nyima's family provide a shared opportunity for them to talk at home about Nyima's school experiences in French or Tibetan. While looking at the pictures together, Nyima can share her memories of the play in her home language as she and her family talk about the photographs. Knowing that developmentally she is likely working on communicating in the past and future tenses in her home language, this strategy supports her current stage of language development.

Home Language Vocabulary Lists

My colleagues and I intentionally integrate meaningful multilingual vocabulary throughout the day. I gather information from multilingual parents about commonly used words and phrases and lists of these words are posted in several places throughout the classroom for us to refer to when we hear children say words in their home language that we don't recognize. During our professional development time before school begins, I orient the teachers to the list and convey the importance of consulting the list to comfort and support children. I also model inserting these words and phrases throughout the day. For example, I use key words and phrases in Kannada for 16-month-old Dhimahee (Table 9.1), Hindi for 18-month-old Remy (Table 9.2), and Spanish for 13-month-old Aman (Table 9.3).

Table 9.1 Vocabulary in Kannada for Dhimahee

Edo	*This one*	*Hopa*	Go
Aatadu	Play	*Hera hopa*	Go outside
Hathu	Climb	*Hopana?*	Shall we go?
Alli	There	*Betu*	I want
Illi	Here	*Beda*	I don't want
Hera	Outside	*Amma mathe bathu.*	Amma will come back later.

Table 9.2 Vocabulary in Hindi for Remy

Dadu	Grandpa	Khaana Khayega? (Kaa-na Ka-ay-ga?)	Do you want to eat?
Dadi	Grandma	Khele ga? (Kaylay gah?)	Do you want to play?
		Pani piye ga? (Pa-knee pee-ay gah?)	Do you want to drink some water?

Table 9.3 Vocabulary in Spanish for Aman

Manos	Hands	Siéntate	Sit down
Brazos	Arms	Rápido	Quickly
Piernas	Legs		

I also build curriculum around children's home experiences, using the voices and words of families. For multilingual children, there is an open invitation for families to share this material with us in their home language, which acknowledges and includes the various languages in our classroom and builds meaningful curriculum for children. We also develop our language and literacy curriculum through (1) letters from family members, (2) classroom created books in which each family member shares an anecdote, and (3) audio recordings of family members reading books or reciting family stories (Table 9.4).

Table 9.4 Home and school language and literacy integration

Teacher Strategies to Engage Across the Ages	Infants	Young Toddlers	Older Toddlers
Letters from Family (Love letter, naptime note) Augment with recordings if teacher doesn't share home language.	Young infants might taste and crumple the paper. Older infants might enjoy seeing their home language scripts and hearing the teacher read the family letters.	Offer materials for young toddlers to draw/write back to the family or offer dictation; repeat their words as you write them down.	Children may tell you what they are writing as they create their own symbols. Repeat what you hear, take dictation or record their words.
Classroom Created Books (Photo and description of a family experience)	Read the description, look at the photo together, and discuss.	Provide materials for children to reenact the experiences described.	Help children notice similarities and differences between children's experiences and languages.
Family Audio Recordings (Song, memory, book)	Children will recognize family voices, familiar words, books, songs in home languages.	Children turn pages along with story and attend to the picture associated with the words; they might sing along with a known song in their home languages.	Children are more interested in their own story and those of their peers; children can discuss story elements and notice language differences.

I work with my colleagues to implement, observe, and document these strategies both within and across each of these age groupings to provide ongoing home-school language integration.

Closing

As a veteran infant-toddler teacher, I have an extensive repertoire of strategies to identify and support children's multilingual learning within my English-medium classroom. I have reached this point through the careful use of inquiry, documentation, and reflection both on my own and with my teaching colleagues. I also attribute my knowledge of ways to support children's multilingualism to ongoing efforts to engage in dialogue and constant communication with families about their languages and their family and cultural identities. I continue to hold the family-child relationship at the center of my work, and value highly responsive relationships with children as the core for supporting multilingual children in my classroom. Helping children to feel seen, heard, valued, and respected in all dimensions of their evolving identities contributes to their Harmonious Bilingualism. Through gathering information, attuned interactions, and designing curriculum I continue to strengthen children's multilingual talents and identities, play preferences, and emotional well-being.

Closing Reflections

1   Which of Seferina's ideas and strategies might you adapt for supporting children's multilingual growth in an infant-toddler classroom?
2   Which of Seferina's ideas and strategies for understanding families' multilingual talents and perspectives are you interested in using in your work?

References

California Department of Social Services. (2020). Child care center general licensing requirements. Retrieved from www.cdss.ca.gov/Portals/9/Regs/7cccman.pdf.

De Houwer, A. (2009). *Bilingual first language acquisition*. Multilingual Matters.

Jones, E., & Nimmo, J. (1994). *Emergent curriculum*. National Association for the Education of Young Children.

Martin, B., & Carle, E. (1992). *Brown bear, bear, what do you see?* Holt.

Weise, A., & Serna, E. (2021). Making meaning together: Connecting with dual language learners in infant and toddler care. Webinar, Program for Infant Toddler Care, May 27. Retrieved from https://vimeo.com/558685663 (accessed December 12, 2021).

WIDA. (2015). Focus on the early years: Observing language use to promote dual language development. Retrieved from https://wida.wisc.edu/sites/default/files/resource/FocusOn-EY-Observing-Language-Use-to-Promote-Dual-Language-Development.pdf (accessed December 12, 2021).

Part IV

Early Literacy

10 Early Literacy Research and Theory on Infants and Toddlers

A Strengths-Based Approach

Mariana Souto-Manning and Crystasany R. Turner

Opening Reflections

1 Which areas of early literacy for infants and toddlers are you most passionate about?
2 What is your vision for a strengths-based approach to the early literacy learning of infants and toddlers?

Every day, infants and toddlers show us—as they point to objects, communicate feelings, and recognize faces, places, and spaces in their homes and communities—that reading "the world always precedes reading the word" (Freire & Macedo, 1987, p. 35). They read faces and places, author relationships, and communicate through coos, babbles, and cries. They author themselves in the world much before authoring themselves via symbols on a page. Yet, restrictive notions of early literacy often devalue the sophisticated communicative practices of children birth to three, and instead focus on "getting ready to read" (Parlakian et al., 2008).

In the early years, *basics* and *readiness* permeate what counts as literacy and educational success. They further reify dominant models of literacy and learning as the norm by which all young children are to be assessed. Thus, young children are rewarded for the alignment between their home and school literacy practices. This approach continues to position minoritized children as unsuccessful, effectively blaming them individually, for society's drive to sustain continued inequity. Here, we argue against discourses of early literacy as being reduced to or prioritizing readiness and "the basics." Instead, we explore how young children take up literacies by drawing from their sociocultural contexts, interactions, and life—across time and space.

Toward Strengths-Based Conceptualizations of Literacy

A strengths-based approach necessitates expansive conceptualizations of early literacy—moving beyond restrictive notions of symbols as letters and of literacy as written words. Although this may appear to be mundane, conceptualizing early literacy is an important undertaking. After all, in the context of early education and society, narrow conceptualizations of literacy delineate lines of inclusion and exclusion, identifying whose language practices and literacies belong and need to be performed.

DOI: 10.4324/9781003227816-15

> **Key Idea**
>
> We conceptualize literacy as making meaning and making sense in/of the world.

Expansive and inclusive conceptualizations of early literacy, though, reject being "enclosed within boundaries" (hooks, 1994, p. 167). In contrast, White, middle-class boundaries delineate traditional notions of early literacy in deeply racialized ways (Souto-Manning et al., 2021).

Early literacy is often understood through a narrow lens of grammar and phonetics around which traditional boundaries are drawn—defining what is and what is not literacy. Contemplating the relationship between language and systems of domination, hooks (1994) underscored: "We must change conventional ways of thinking about language, creating spaces where diverse voices can speak" (p. 226). Likewise, conventional thinking about early literacy delimits whose voices are centered and whose are marginalized along axes of oppression (Collins, 1990).

"Shifting how we think about language and how we use it necessarily alters how we know what we know" (hooks, 1994, p. 226)—and so does shifting the way we think about literacy. This limited and limiting understanding negates the rich literacy practices brought to classrooms by multilingual children who are Black, Indigenous, and of Color and whose communicative practices do not mirror "academic language," a cloak for White English (Baker-Bell, 2020). This understanding ignores children's prior engagement and participation in "a storytelling tradition, that may include listening to and recounting oral histories, parables, stories (cuentos) and proverbs (dichos)" and fails to recognize associated literacy skills of "memorization, attention to detail, dramatic pauses, comedic timing, facial affect, vocal tone, volume, rhythm and rhyme" (Yosso, 2005, pp. 78–79).

Early Literacy

From infancy, through coos, babbles, cries, smiles, gestures, movements, and words, young children author themselves in/and their worlds (Souto-Manning & Yoon, 2018). They make sense of their world, use symbols, and develop their literate practices and identities. Young children may start reading and labeling all animals similarly—and may say "dog," "woof-woof," "pero," "guau-guau," "cachorro," "au-au," or another descriptor or sound typical of a dog when they see a mammal (e.g. a cat, a lion, or a hippopotamus). In doing so, they make sense of a symbol system, using one utterance to refer to animals, and more precisely to mammals. Eventually, they differentiate between the different kinds of animals and mammals, for example, using cat, lion, and hippo to signify different mammals. Thus, it is essential for early educators to understand how young children are always in process as they develop their early literacies.

Instead of imposing one-size-fits-all conceptualizations, expectations, or benchmarks delineating literacy, early childhood educators should engage in learning from young children's literacy practices. Failing to do so is not only inadequate—taking into account the role of context and relationships in early literacy development—but problematically imposes a restrictive conceptualization of literacy as a yardstick for all children's literacy development, Eurocentrically excluding children whose literacy practices do not align with "the settled expectations of relative white privilege as a legitimate and natural baseline" (Harris, 1993, p. 1714).

Restrictive notions of literacy position young children in terms of what they cannot do (constructing deficits), a Eurocentric view of literacy that often inflicts harm. It upholds White ways of making meaning and making sense in the world, and White English, as "the legitimation of expectations of power and control that enshrine the status quo as a neutral baseline, while masking the maintenance of white privilege and domination" (Harris, 1993, p. 1715). This results in the entanglement of Whiteness and what is deemed academic literacy and language practices (Baker-Bell, 2020), at the detriment of the social, emotional, and psychological well-being of children of Color and of children whose literacy practices do not match the settled expectations of Whiteness. After all, the literacy practices of power are ultimately the literacy practices of those who have power in society (Delpit, 2006).

Pressing on the acquisition of racialized notions of literacy practice—which ascribe belonging under the label of "academic"—excludes children whose families and communities have been historically disempowered through societal divestments. Such pressures often frame young children who are Black, Indigenous, and of Color as already behind before they are born. Young children whose family and community communicative practices do not align with White English or academic language (Baker-Bell, 2020) often yearn to belong in school and/or are encouraged to approximate and perform Whiteness via the performance of expected literacy practices in ways detrimental to their development. Suspending the social, emotional, and psychological harm sponsored by traditional conceptualizations of literacy, which orient to a White compass (Souto-Manning & Yoon, 2018), requires a deep examination of literacy that centers the strengths, cultivates the brilliance, and sustains the ingenuity of young children who are Black, Indigenous, and of Color (Delpit, 2012).

Early literacy cannot continue to be defined by the mere acquisition of specific skills, but must be (re)defined; early literacy must honor, cultivate and sustain multiple positionalities, points of view, and ways of making sense in and of the world—as a matter of belonging.

Key Idea

Early literacy must honor, cultivate and sustain multiple positionalities, points of view, and ways of making sense in and of the world—as a matter of belonging.

Early literacy can be expanded as educators and researchers embrace a stance of humility, (re)positioning themselves as learners, and genuinely seeking to understand the literacy practices of children engaged in literacy practices that entail breaking through the encapsulation of named languages (e.g., "English," "Spanish," "Arabic," "Chinese," "Swahili," "Russian," and "Haitian Creole"), all of which delineate "socially invented categories" with "real and material effects" (García & Kleyn, 2016, pp. 1, 10). Instead of emphasizing so-called "basic skills," conceptualized as problems of the individual, we must reconceptualize early literacy—in expansive, inclusive and plural ways that draw on strengths-based theories.

Strengths-Based Theories of Early Literacy

We take a strengths-based approach to early literacy, and briefly explore six areas of literacy that cultivate the ingenuity of young children, families, and communities—especially those who are Black, Indigenous, and of Color. We draw on Larson and Marsh's (2015) delineations of these theoretical traditions of literacy:

- *New literacy studies* conceptualize literacy as "a critical social practice constructed in everyday interactions across local contexts" (p. 2).
- *Critical literacy* "involves interrogating texts in terms of the power relations embedded within and reflected by them, in addition to positioning readers and authors as active agents in text creation and analysis" (p. 3).
- *Digital literacies* attend to how literacy practices are mediated by technologies and how these technologies are transforming the very foundations of literacy into *new literacies*, "practices that arise from the relationship between literacy and technologies" (p. 3).
- *Spatial literacies* attend to how space and time are entangled with and impact literacy practices in a range of ways, especially considering the complex relationship of literacy and play across domains—e.g., offline, online.
- *Multimodal and artifactual literacies* focus on communicative practices that involve a wide range of modes and media, attending to "the way in which material objects are inscribed into literacy practices" (p. 3).
- *Sociocultural literacy* "challenges traditional definitions of learning as the transmission of knowledge" and (re)defines literacy learning and development "as changing participation in culturally valued activity with more expert others" (p. 3)—regardless of whether these more expert others are adults or peers.

Below, we explore early literacies—focusing on birth to three—and explore examples that bring more expansive conceptualizations to life.

Early Literacies: Birth to Three

Infants from birth to 12 months learn and develop through embodied and relational literacies. They make their mark in the world by showing their feelings and (at times intentions) via sounds, facial expressions, and body movements. Some infants communicate via signs and/or sign language, and engage in communicative practices that traverse the boundaries delineating languages. It is important for caregivers and family members to engage with them by interacting, responding, talking, and making movements and facial expressions. Babies also learn by playing, moving, and experimenting. From the earliest years, they enjoy being told stories orally and can be socialized into enjoying books, even attempting to turn pages (which, may end up being torn ... but it's all part of the process!).

Although infants' communications may not be clear or understandable to us adults at first, when they cry, make sounds, make facial expressions, and move their arms, legs, and other parts of their bodies, they engage in communicating—making meaning and making sense of and in the world. This is the beginning of literacy. As caregivers, it is important to attend to their patterns to learn what infants mean, reaffirm their communicative efforts by responding to their communicative attempts and signals, and view their literacy development as happening in varied culturally situated ways.

Most babies babble a lot starting at about three months. When someone talks, they engage, talk back and make lots of sounds back. At this time, babies develop receptive language. They listen to those around them. Some adults copy the sounds babies make, extending the conversation in a way that is aligned with the improv technique of "yes and." Later, adults can support language practices and literacy development translanguaging. By example, in his young toddler classroom, 25-month-old Matthew "picked up three purple water beads and stated that they were '小蜜蜂' or 'Xiǎo mìfēng' (little bee)." One of the adults in the classroom "asked Matthew in Mandarin to elaborate some more and he said they were 'a grape,' this time responding to Claire's question in English" (Souto-Manning et al., 2022, p. 7).

Another example is that of an interaction between Jenna (22 months old) and her mother at bedtime "in Jenna's quiet, dimly lit bedroom" (Lindfors, 2008, p. 25):

MOTHER: So, Jenna, did you have a busy day today [at daycare]?
JENNA: Paydo.
MOTHER: Did you play with playdough today, Jenna?
JENNA: Geen.
MOTHER: You played with green playdough?
JENNA: Yeah. Marta [her daycare teacher].
MOTHER: Yes. You play with playdough with Marta.

In the first few months, infants start to figure out how things work, exploring their own bodies (with hands, mouth, eyes). Because literacies develop relationally, it is really important to play with infants, find books, objects, and toys that they can explore (making sounds, bringing it to their mouth), and engage in singing, storytelling and playing games like peek-a-boo.

For hearing babies, one of the first literacies they develop is the ability to recognize the voices of their caregivers. Because literacy is relational, physical closeness further develops literacy—sitting baby in the lap, cuddling with baby by swaddling them with textiles against a caregiver's body. By the time babies are one, they are likely saying one or two words. Those words are heavily informed by the language practices in which they are socialized.

Young toddlers (12–24 months) use sounds, actions and movements to communicate and make their mark in the world, communicating what they are feeling. They use signs as well. It is important for caregivers to understand the sounds, utterances, and signals young children employ instead of expecting young children to comply to expected literacy practices. Importantly, young toddlers draw on their entire linguistic repertoire (across named languages) to communicate. When their communicative efforts are understood, supported, welcomed, and validated, they take risks and develop their babbles into intelligible words. Nevertheless, it can be hard to understand what young toddlers are saying; in these instances (and others), caregivers of young toddlers should learn from family and community members and from the toddlers themselves.

Young toddlers understand more words than they can express or speak. For example, in Tara Lencl's toddler classroom, 2-year-old Martina plays at the water table and her peers stand on towels typically used to catch any overflowing water. Martina approaches her teacher, Tara, relying on her full communicative repertoire to make meaning and communicate. Martina states: "Necesito … necesito … this one" as she points "at the towel her friend was standing on" to which Tara responds "Oh! You need a towel!" Without missing a beat, Martina says "Necesito towel" (Genishi & Lencl, 2015, p. 282). After Tara hands a towel to Martina, she utters the word "towel" as she spreads the towel on the floor by the water table and stands on it. "Martina draws on her knowledge of both Spanish and English" (p. 282), as named languages, to communicate.

Telling stories about objects and artifacts can also develop one's understanding about young toddlers' communication and support their expressive language. Here, caregivers can cultivate space for young toddlers to take the lead, although this can be difficult especially because young toddlers tend to express strong opinions, which might challenge adult preferences. Although adults might feel compelled to manage such opinions with options (this or that?), such choices can result in exclusion and be culturally insensitive, as visible in the exchange between Emmy (toddler teacher) and Thomas (20-month-old).

> After play time, Emmy asked Thomas: "Would you like to clean up?" Thomas responded: "No." Emmy thought it was funny that Thomas had said no, and shared this interaction with his mother. That evening, Thomas's mother mentioned the interaction to him, explaining that his response may have been understood as rude or impolite. On the very next day, when Emmy asked Thomas if he'd like to clean up, he proudly said: "No, thank you!"

Although Thomas had revised his response after his interaction with his mother, adding "thank you!" to the response "No," "No, thank you!" did not align with norms of politeness in dominant US society, whereby such questions in effect signify polite requests and are not really meant as questions. Yet, because in his home, questions did not signal requests, but questions, Thomas employed his prior literacy practice (developed within the context of his home where directness was the norm) in school. His response in this new context is likely to be understood as an affront or refusal, an inappropriate response to the request which had been politely made by his teacher. Nevertheless, it was the appropriate response within the context of his home.

Older toddlers (24–36 months) start to engage in the authorship process through play. Although this authorship process may not encompass writing symbols on a page, it entails conceptualizing a story, developing a storyline, considering setting, characters, and interactions, and along the way, revising the story as needed. They are also starting to understand if-then clauses in real life to test hypotheses. For example, 30-month-old Antonio, despite being told by his father that it was cold outside and he needed a coat, resisted putting on his coat until he got outside and felt the cold.

In addition to testing hypotheses, older toddlers engage in problem solving (unrolling the entire roll of paper towels to clean a spill), and are often practicing by doing the same thing again and again—whether watching an episode of *Daniel Tiger's Neighborhood* or *Doc McStuffins* dozens of times or repeating the same action with a toy. This repetition—a subject of both speculation and exasperation by adults—allows older toddlers to practice and to learn. Older toddlers at times bring some of the episodes they have watched dozens of times to life in their play and incorporate particular phrases or expressions in their everyday talk. Also the subject of some adult exasperation, older toddlers also ask *why?*—a lot! Although their questions may appear inconsequential—Why are there so many stars in the sky? Why do I have to put my coat on? Why does it take so long for grandmomma?—these questions signal their theorizations about the world around them. This means that they are not relying on taken-for-granted assumptions, but are developing their critical literacy practices, questioning status quo understanding and assumptions, and pursuing questions and potentialities such as "what if?" and "why?"

Older toddlers may also start making marks on a page—with crayon, markers, or other objects. This can be encouraged by setting up opportunities for their markings to make meaning. This may entail, for example, implementing a mail system in a preschool classroom with mailboxes and encouraging young children to author letters. For instance, in Phillip Baumgarner's Head Start classroom, although the children were not yet writing in conventional ways, they made marks on paper that acted as forms of communicative exchanges with their peers (Souto-Manning, 2010). In this classroom, the "children engaged in written conversations through art notes, using mailboxes and written correspondence delivered daily by one of the children" (Souto-Manning & Martell, 2016, pp. 16–17). Encouraging and validating older toddlers' writing (even when they may seem like scribbles) and drawing builds their identity and confidence as writers. Ultimately, early literacies produce and/or reproduce identities.

Overall, research has increasingly shown that infants and toddlers are highly competent symbol-makers and symbol-users in home, community, and educational settings. They are motivated to explore and engage with varied print and digital literacies in constructive and synergistic collaboration with peers, siblings, intergenerational family members, and educators. In this sociocultural process, cultural values and traditions are influenced by family and community literacy practices; intergenerational perspectives delineate forms and functions of literacy.

A Strengths-Based Approach to Supporting Young Children's Literacies

Foundational to a strengths-based approach to supporting young children's literacy is the belief that *every* child has strengths. This belief guides us as we seek to learn from and about their literacies, listening to their stories and voices, and connecting with them. To do so in an authentic and foundational way, we must observe and document their literacy practices, focusing on what they can do, how they participate in many communities within our classroom and beyond, and making sure that our teaching builds on their strengths.

Despite an all-too-common focus on what children lack—their deficits and risks—young children have diverse and sophisticated literacy repertoires.

Key Idea

Despite an all-too-common focus on what children lack—their deficits and risks—young children have diverse and sophisticated literacy repertoires.

Instead of measuring children's language and literacy practices against settled expectations of literacy benchmarks that uphold White-centric practices and (re)produce deficits, we can understand how young children's rich language and literacy repertoires develop through a variety of social, historical, and cultural tools and activities. Given the time, space, and opportunity, children will share their language and literacy repertoires and the myriad ways in which they are capable and knowledgeable. We can also learn about children's literacies from their families, expanding our understanding of early literacies. Funds of knowledge serve as a way of engaging in this learning.

Expanding Early Literacies through Funds of Knowledge

To engage in expansive conceptualizations of early literacies, we have to make ourselves vulnerable and recognize that "No one knows it all, no one is ignorant of everything" (Freire, 2005, p. 72). This stance allows us to learn how families and communities "contribute another layer of influence to children's literacy" practices, and how "different families and different cultural groups stress different kinds of activities, knowledge, uses of language, values, work, social interactions, and social organization" (Owocki & Goodman, 2002, p. 5). Their unique literacy histories can be gleaned via funds of knowledge—the "historically accumulated and culturally developed bodies of knowledge essential for household or individual functioning and well-being" (Moll et al., 1992, p. 133), including household management (childcare, cooking), economics (sales), material and scientific knowledge (construction), medicine (herbal knowledge, folk cures), and more. Importantly, funds of knowledge position young children and their families as skillful and resourceful, offering a potent pathway for redefining early literacies expansively.

Funds of knowledge can (re)position young children, and unsettle traditional power arrangements and power-laden relationships between their own literacies and those (over) valued in schools and society. They can help us re-mediate early literacies. This is an important undertaking, as young children, families, and communities who are Black, Indigenous, and of Color and whose literacies are not aligned with the literacy of power (over)valued in early childhood are often viewed as needing remediation. Instead, the pedagogical counterstory below offers insights into how the very notion of early literacies needs re-mediation (adapted from Souto-Manning & Yoon, 2018):

> After observing children play "boiling" pretend plants in a pot on the stove, serving peers healing medicine, Ms. Pio recognized a common fund of knowledge: herbal remedies. Centering this fund of knowledge, Ms. Pio read *My Tata's Remedies* by Rivera-Ashford aloud. Although this was a longer book, it resonated with the children, who were attentive, occasionally looking at the book and at each other, making silent text-to-self connections. The children were familiar with natural healing remedies, part of their cultural repertoires in the neighborhood and families. The book reflected their fund of knowledge: when they got sick, they often took herbal remedies. Many had family members who had long relied on the botanica and its medicinal herbs and plants, candles, incense, and other health and religious items to heal. As such, their literacies were quite developed as they talked about the book and (re)designed an area of their classroom as a botanica.

This example shows how, since learning and literacies are relational and contextual endeavors, experiences more meaningful to young children often result in deeper learning, offering important implications for reimagining and retheorizing literacies more expansively and justly.

Conclusion

The literacies of young children who are Black, Indigenous, and of Color cannot and should not be understood against White-centric and normative literacy conceptualizations and practices. Such delimiting of early literacies harms young children from birth, sponsoring assimilation and erasure. Here, to suspend harm, we call for early literacies to better reflect Black, Indigenous, and other young children of Color's ability to develop and draw upon various language registers and styles to communicate with different listeners.

We also recognize the power of early literacies co-constructed within the context of everyday interactions, taking place across contexts (bedroom, kitchen, playground, classroom, FaceTiming with abuela in Mexico), and at times mediated by technology. From birth, infants and toddlers cross borders between literacies, named languages, spaces, and domains. The professional development process of questioning sedimented notions of literacy—and challenging relations of authority, hierarchy, and power—repositions young children as active agents in reading, authoring, and responding to texts.

Infants and toddlers develop their own early literacies alongside peers, family and community members in culturally valued and situated activities, which may sponsor the resignification of symbols to reflect children's funds of knowledge. As we collaborate to reconceptualize and theorize early literacies more expansively, may we remember that young children "make the best theorists, since they...do not yet grasp our social practices as inevitable, they do not see why we might not do things differently" (Eagleton, 1990, p. 34). As powerful theorists and brilliant resignifiers, they operate outside of the limited and limiting constructs of early literacy, inviting us to constantly reread and rewrite our own conceptualizations of early literacies in ever more expansive and inclusive ways. It is up to us to follow their lead.

Closing Reflections

1   Based on this chapter, how do you see children's funds of knowledge and their sociocultural talents influencing their early literacy learning from birth?
2   What new ideas and strategies do you now want to implement based upon this chapter's discussion of ways to support the early literacy learning of young children who are Black, Indigenous, and of Color?

References

Baker-Bell, A. (2020). *Linguistic justice*. Routledge.

Collins, P. H. (1990). Black feminist thought in the matrix of domination. *Black Feminist Thought*, 138, 221–238.

Delpit, L. (2006). *Other people's children*. The New Press.

Delpit, L. (2012). *"Multiplication is for white people": Raising expectations for other people's children*. The New Press.

Eagleton, T. (1990). *The significance of theory*. Blackwell.

Freire, P. (2005). *Teachers as cultural workers*. Taylor & Francis.

Freire, P., & Macedo, D. (1987). *Literacy: Reading the word and the world*. Bergin & Garvey.

García, O., & Kleyn, T. (2016). Translanguaging theory in education. In O. García & T. Kleyn (Eds.), *Translanguaging with multilingual students* (pp. 9–33). Routledge.

Genishi, C., & Lencl, T. (2015). "My mommy doesn't speak English": Supporting children as emergent bilinguals. In L. J. Couse & S. L. Recchia (Eds.), *Handbook of early childhood teacher education* (pp. 291–305). Routledge.

Harris, C. (1993). Whiteness as property. *Harvard Law Review*, 106(8), 1707–1791.

hooks, b. (1994). *Teaching to transgress*. Routledge.

Larson, J., & Marsh, J. (2015). *Making literacy real*. Sage.

Lindfors, J. (2008). *Children's language*. Teachers College Press.

Moll, L., Amanti, C., Neff, D., & Gonzalez, N. (1992). Funds of knowledge for teaching: Using a qualitative approach to connect homes and classrooms. *Theory into Practice*, 31(2), 132–141.

Owocki, G. & Goodman, Y. (2002). *Kidwatching*. Heinemann.

Parlakian, R., Lerner, C., & Im, J. (2008). *Getting ready to read*. Zero to Three.

Souto-Manning, M. (2010). Challenging ethnocentric literacy practices: [Re]positioning home literacies in a head start classroom. *Research in the Teaching of English*, 45(2), 150–178.

Souto-Manning, M., & Martell, J. (2016). *Reading, writing, and talk: Inclusive teaching strategies for diverse learners*. Teachers College Press.

Souto-Manning, M., & Yoon, H. (2018). *Rethinking early literacies: Reading and rewriting worlds*. Routledge.

Souto-Manning, M., Ghim, H., & Madu, N. (2021). Toward early literacy as a site of belonging. *The Reading Teacher*, 74(5), 483–492.

Souto-Manning, M., Martell, J., Pérez, A., & Pión, P. (2022). Translanguaging as norm: Rejecting narrow and restrictive notions of reading. *The Reading Teacher*, 75(3), 339–350. doi:10.1002/trtr.2022.

Yosso, T. (2005). Whose culture has capital? A critical race theory discussion of community cultural wealth. *Race, Ethnicity and Education*, 8(1), 69–91.

11 Using Children's Books for Sensory Exploration and Language Learning

Cheryl Horney

Opening Reflections

1   What do you see as the most important elements and strategies for supporting the early book exploration of infants and toddlers?
2   What challenges and issues have you experienced in selecting child and culturally responsive books and stories for young children, and how do you want to strengthen this process for you and your colleagues?

Eleven-month-old Ethan lays on his stomach on the floor of a public library reading a board book with colors and flaps alongside his father Patrick. Ethan reaches out with his left hand and flips the page, wiggling his legs and hands in excitement as his father says "purple" with a big smile. Ethan stares at the book while kicking his legs with excitement. "What's this one?" Patrick asks. Ethan reaches out and flips the flap with his right hand. Patrick says "pink" with a smile. Ethan wiggles his hands and feet with joy as he looks at the page (Figure 11.1).

Infants and toddlers explore everything around them in their communities, parks, sidewalks, homes, classrooms and everywhere in between. They move in and out of play exploring sounds, symbols, and pictures in their worlds. As adults we support these discoveries through providing a pathway for young children to develop a love of literacy with their body and their minds. As a former infant-toddler teacher, current program director for a locally, state and federally funded program in San Francisco and the mother of a two-year-old, I've had the opportunity to witness this exploration from many perspectives. Our program serves twelve Early Learning Centers throughout San Francisco. We also operate a home visiting program for pregnant women and children 0–3 which sends an Infant/Toddler and Family Specialist into the home of a family on a weekly basis to work with the dyad of the child and parent to support the parent as the child's primary educator. We serve a diverse population of children and families who speak various home languages and represent different cultures and backgrounds.

In this chapter, I focus on the power of books for infant-toddler language and literacy learning based upon my experiences as a teacher and administrator, as well as my conversations with eight experienced infant-toddler colleagues. They all have worked with infants and toddlers in our program for over 5 years and have at least 10 years of experience working in the field with infants and toddlers. The colleagues are Merced Rocha, Leshanti Smith, Gloria Redenius, Martha Ly, Tiffany Zeng, Yingshan (Lisa) Li, Tamila Branner, and Keyla Canales.

DOI: 10.4324/9781003227816-16

Figure 11.1 Ethan and father read a book together through nonverbal and verbal communication

Book Selection: Considering Development, Culture, and Language

Children can see, touch, smell, listen to, and even taste books if they're selected appropriately. According to Schickedanz (1999), "babies interact with books differently than do older children, even very young babies like books and engage with them in rather remarkable ways" (p. 11). Young infants (0–6 months) don't always explore books the way we think they should. Infants first show interest in books through grabbing, mouthing and turning the pages of books. They then start to point and name pictures in books, and sit for varied periods of time on their own as they look at and physically interact with books (Mangione & Greenwald, 2011). Adult-initiated reading provides opportunities for visual and tactile stimulation and for conversation and social bond development. For example, my partner and I read dozens of books to Ethan as we held him close and rocked him. He would not look at the pages of the book but rather stared up into our faces and watched us as we spoke — "At this young age shared reading is at its core, about the social experience of connecting with others through language" (Schickedanz & Collins, 2013, p. 21).

Books for infants and toddlers provide children with full sensory experiences. These books are especially made for durability, such as stiff cardboard books, which are often designed specifically for small infants' and toddlers' hands. There are books with flaps, mirrors, textures and sound makers to further deepen infants' sensory experiences. There are also more indestructible books made from vinyl and non-toxic materials that allow infants to turn pages on their own without ripping them. Young children love to crinkle, pull, turn, mouth, and squeeze all of these different types of books. Having a variety of types and materials of books in all classrooms allows each child to individualize their literacy experiences, and allows teachers and families to use particular books to match children's interests and talents. In selecting books, we consider a number of child development milestones as linked with specific language and literacy elements of the books (Table 11.1).

In our centers, we also uphold children's and families' cultures and home languages as vital for their identities and sense of well-being (Mangione & Greenwald, 2011). Books help children explore their identity and accept and respect the diversity of others (Birckmayer et al., 2008). When selecting books to use in our classrooms, my colleagues and I consider all aspects of children's identities, including family size and structure, home languages, and home cultures. We use certain criteria for book selection and for documenting and reflecting

Table 11.1 Important book features for infants and toddlers

Age Range	Book Features
Birth to 6 months	• Vinyl, plastic, cloth, books with fold out flaps • Stiff cardboard books (board books) • Large, bright simple designs with contrasting backgrounds • One picture or photograph per page • Black and white contrast • Nursery rhymes and verse books Suggested books: *Baby Faces Series*, Roberta Grobel Intrater; *Black on White*, Tana Hoban; *Cradle Me*, Debby Slier
7–12 months	• Cardboard books • Simple and realistic drawings • Bright and bold illustrations • Photographs of faces • Rhymes and songs Suggested books: *Global Babies /Bebes del Mundo*, A Global Fund for Children book; *Twinkle Twinkle Small Hōkū*, Jing Jing Tsong; *Whose Toes Are Those?*, Jabari Asmi
13–18 months	• Handles • Stiff or plastic-coated pages • Flaps • Contain familiar items: people, food, animals • Repetitive verses Suggested books: *Busy Fingers*, C. W. Bowie; *My Very First Book of Food*, Eric Carle; *More, More, More Said the Baby*, Vera B. Williams
19–26 months	• Pictures on every page • Children as the main characters • Contain familiar items: animals, everyday objects • Contain plots and characters Suggested books: *Mommy, Mama, and Me*, Leslea Newman; *Woke Baby*, Mahogany L. Browne; *Fiesta Babies*, Carmen Tafolla
27–36 months	• Concept books • Board books • Picture books • Song books • Rhyming books Suggested books: *Cerca/Close*, Juan Felipe Herrera; *Bringing in the New Year*, Grace Lin; *Anti Racist Baby*, Ibram X. Kendi

Sources: This chart borrowed extensively from Birckmayer, Kennedy, & Stonehouse (2008), Schickedanz (1999), and Schickedanz & Collins (2013), as well as infant/toddler educator interviews with Tamila Branner, Keyla Canales, Yingshan (Lisa) Li, Martha Ly, Gloria Redenius Merced Rocha, Leshanti Smith, and Tiffany Zeng

on the benefits of the books for children's language and literacy growth from infancy through toddlerhood (Table 11.2).

In addition to carefully choosing child and culturally responsive books in the classrooms, our "home visitor" staff visit children and families in their homes and share book exploration experiences, where we encourage children to take the lead (Figure 11.2).

Table 11.2 Criteria for child and culturally responsive book selection

Diversity and Identity

- Does this book represent the identities of the children in my classroom?
- Is this book inclusive of the children in my classroom?
- Does this book introduce other identities to my classroom?

Language

- Is this book in the home languages of children in my classroom?
- Is this book in English and the home language?
- Who can I invite to read this book to our class?
- When reading the book are we pronouncing words correctly?

Culture

- Is the book representative of the traditions, holidays, and practices of the families and children in my classroom?
- Are the clothes and customs displayed relatable to the families in the classroom?
- Is the book absent of bias and stereotypes?
- Is this a book that the families in my classroom would want to read to their child or have recommended?
- Does this book represent family situations that are familiar to the children in my classroom?

Authorship and Illustrations

- Is this book written by an author that is part of the culture they are sharing?
- Do I have books from different authors and with different styles of illustrations?
- Are the illustrations vibrant and realistic?
- Are the illustrations absent of bias and stereotypes?

Interest

- Does this book contain something that my child is interested in?

Accessing Multicultural and Multilingual Children's Books

Our centers leverage various community resources to help us support our children's and families' literacy practices and to help us access diverse books:

- local public libraries;
- book mobiles;
- book donation programs;
- book sharing programs;
- Little Free Libraries; and
- digital resources.

Local libraries are powerful community resources, often staffed by children's librarians who are passionate about suggesting developmentally, linguistically, and culturally relevant books for young children. When reflecting on the access provided by our local library, another of our staff members recounted:

> One year, a newcomer mother who didn't have books at home for her child, preferred to buy him toys. I scheduled our next meeting at the library, and I showed the mother ways she can read a book to her child even without knowing how to read. The mother asked me to bring books to the child at every meeting, and they got a library

Figure 11.2 A child takes the lead in reading

card and went to the library twice a week, and joined the library's play group in her home language and borrowed books to take home.

Our centers also utilize the traveling bookmobile vans sponsored by the public library and our staff support our children and families during book selection. We also participate in book donation programs like San Francisco's Children's Book Project, national and local book sharing programs that provide multilingual book bags for families, and community-based book exchanges facilitated by the eight Little Free Libraries we built at our Family Child Care sites. The children love the Little Free Libraries and they can reach in for books, exchange them, and bring books home and keep them (Figure 11.3).

While our centers prioritize promoting access to physical books for our children and families, we also are committed to sharing digital resources that may be more easily accessible to our families. Guided by the recommendation of the American Academy of Pediatrics (2021) that children under 18 months avoid screen time and that children between 18 months and 24 months engage in limited amounts of high-quality online storytelling content, we suggest that families who do watch online read-alouds or use e-books do so with their children and discuss the content and stories together. Our centers also use various digital platforms and resources to research books that represent our children and families, access hard-to-find books, and share photos and observations that document our children's literacy journeys.

Exploring Books with Infants and Toddlers at School and Home

Our centers employ various strategies to engage infants and toddlers in literary experiences (Table 11.3).

While we utilize specific strategies more often for certain age groups of children (e.g. hold young infants in our arms while we explore a book), we also use other certain strategies for all children across the age span (e.g. creating ample spaces for children to see and access books). We also work with families to encourage them to use as many of these book exploration strategies as they can at home and in community settings. These strategies recognize families' linguistic and cultural capital, and share the common goal of

Figure 11.3 A child using a Little Free Library (https://littlefreelibrary.org)

empowering families to feel confident and knowledgeable in engaging with their young children with books and stories.

Telling Stories

Yingshan (Lisa) Li, a Home Visitor, uses a storytelling strategy with families who speak Chinese and have difficulty finding books in their home language. Yingshan encourages families to use the pictures in their available books to create their own stories that represent their culture and language. There are also many wordless books that tell stories through the illustrations, and the children and adults co-create their own storyline in their languages of choice as well as use nonverbal communication such as gesture. These strategies help address a barrier that some families experience in not feeling confident in their ability to read fluently. By focusing on home language storytelling, educators and families can work together to affirm rich cultural and language traditions and practices. We also encourage families to tell traditional stories with props, photos, and music to invite even more sensory engagement for children. Examples of books that lend themselves well to storytelling include *Brown Bear, Brown Bear* (Carle & Martin, 1997), *Besos for Baby* (Arena & Gomez, 2014), *The Snowy Day* (Keats, 1962), *Mama, Do You Love Me?* (Joosse & Lavallee, 1991), and *Dreamers* (Morales, 2018). For family members who don't know traditional stories, we remind them that infants and toddlers are often interested in simple stories about everyday things involving familiar people, places, or things.

Sharing Social Stories

The creation of a social story for a child can be read and shared both at home and school. A social story is a story designed for an individual child or group of children

Table 11.3 Strategies for exploring books with children 0–36 months

Age	Strategies for Exploring Books
0–6 months	One on one engagement with young infants Stay close to infants and at their eye level Hold infants in your arms on the floor, in a chair or rocker Engage infants through varied voice intonations and eye contact so they feel that books are a comforting experience Point and label items Put books in a basket or box on the floor and allow infants to have tummy time to reach and grab books
7–12 months	Sit and share books together Older mobile infants/young toddlers may enjoy soft materials such as cozy blankets and stuffed animals Have books available throughout the classroom at all times of the day Introduce multilingual books During free play one teacher can sit in the book area to read books to children who come by Use these steps to interact with infants as you read: 1 Engage children by saying "Look" and "See that." 2 Ask "What's That?" and "What do you see?." 3 Wait a few seconds for infants to vocalize and if necessary answer yourself. 4 Acknowledge and provide feedback to children (Schickedanz, 1999, p. 21). Respond to children's vocalizations and co-construct "conversations" about the books
13–24 months	Continue having books available all throughout the day Create a cozy corner or book nook for infants and toddlers to crawl or for a toddler to reach and grab books Allow children to sit in your lap as you read to them Individual reading or very small groups are most effective Older infants and toddlers may want to read the same book over and over again Use felt or secure hooks for children to take photos off and on the wall and hold Read books featuring simple questions that children can respond to Continue to ask questions and engage in co-constructed conversations Photocopy or draw book characters and place them around the classroom to start conversations with children Sing songs about the books using different tones and cadences
25–36 months	Continue to have books available in classroom areas and at all times of the day Encourage children to choose books to read Talk to young toddlers about taking care of books Share stories accompanied by physical actions and action language games Support acting out stories and creating oral stories Use puppets and other props to extend and build on books Encourage drawing and artistic connections to books

Sources: This chart borrowed extensively from Birckmayer, Kennedy, & Stonehouse (2008), Schickedanz (1999), and Schickedanz & Collins (2013), as well as infant/toddler educator interviews with Tamila Branner, Keyla Canales, Yingshan (Lisa) Li, Martha Ly, Gloria Redenius Merced Rocha, Leshanti Smith, and Tiffany Zeng

about their routines such as nap time, going to or from school, or playing with friends (Hughes, 2009). My colleagues create social stories with large photos and simple words to tell the story of a child's routine. For infants and toddlers, a social story ideally includes real photographs of the child, their families and their routines for the child to feel a sense of belonging and connection to the story. For example, on the second day of school, one child's eyes lit up and they dried their tears as they pointed to the transition social story that they had been reading with their family. These stories are accessible to the children in the classrooms and copies are sent home for children to share with families.

Book Making with Families and Classroom Family Books

Keyla Canales, another Home Visitor, supports our families and educators to build their libraries with culturally and linguistically representative books by making their own. In certain languages, even well-intentioned mass-produced translations use words that do not correspond to a particular family's regional dialect. In making our own books, Keyla recommends looking for magazine images, printed photos, or for adults to create their own pictures and use simple words to create the books. Infants and young toddlers can see the photos and feel the paper, and point to their favorite pictures. The photos can be placed in sheet protectors, lamination, or contact paper and bound with a large key ring so that infants can interact with the book on their own and with peers.

Creating books about children and their families also helps all families feel welcome in classrooms. As a teacher, when I first met a family, I would ask their permission to take their family photo, which I then printed out and laminated for each family. After I printed and laminated the photos, I would place them together with a large key ring so children could peruse them as often as they wished. I usually made multiple copies of the book and placed them in different areas of the classroom. Many of our younger toddlers grab the key ring and carry the book around the classroom and even outside for looking at on their own or with peers.

Food and Nap Time Routines

Food, found in many books such as *Dim Sum for Everyone* (Lin, 2001) and *Let's Eat! ¡A Comer!* (Mora, 2008), is a great entry point for exploring culture through all the senses. With young infants, food and cooking experiences can include showing them pictures and relating those pictures to their current diet. For older infants and younger toddlers, they can make connections to books that show pictures of fruit and vegetables, and then we can cut up the food for children to touch, taste, smell and hear. In another sensory connection, we create routines before nap time such as using the rocking chair to read a book while rocking young infants to sleep. This calming moment to connect is also a routine that families can enjoy at home before going to sleep.

Songs

Martha Ly, mother of a newborn and former infant/toddler educator, preserves her home language by singing songs in Chinese with her daughter. We also invite families into our classrooms to share songs they sing at home and that are important to their culture, and we set up routines to sing these new culturally relevant songs in different languages. The traditional rhythm of songs for our youngest learners are often easy to learn, and when singing songs in other languages we make sure that we have a native language speaker to guide us in the pronunciation of the words. Children are also often comforted by the familiarity of books based on children's songs accompanied by music on a CD or links to music online. When we can't find these books, we make them using simple pictures to represent the lyrics. Some examples of lyrical books that I like to read with infants and toddlers include *Barnyard Dance* (Boynton, 2017), *Busy Toes* (Bowey & Willingham, 2000), and *Twinkle, Twinkle Small Hoku* (Tsong, 2013).

Conclusion

In this chapter, I discussed multiple perspectives and approaches to invite young children to begin their literacy journeys with books. I highlighted helpful ways to select developmentally appropriate and multicultural and multilingual books for young children. I also discussed effective routines that my colleagues use to intentionally plan environments and strategies for book sharing, sensory exploration, discussion, and storytelling. A key element of creating powerful connections to books also involves families, and affirming their languages, cultures, and literacy practices and knowledge to help set a solid foundation for children's lifelong love of books.

Closing Reflections

1 In looking again at Table 11.3, which of these strategies do you already use as an educator? Which ones would you like to try out and observe how well they work?
2 What do you find appealing about Cheryl and her colleagues' use of social stories, the Free Little Libraries, and other approaches? How might you adopt and adapt these approaches in your work with children and families?

Useful Resources

Book Donation Programs

- Bridge of Books (https://bridgeofbooksfoundation.org)—Provides books to families and programs throughout new Jersey.
- Children's Book Project (www.childrensbookproject.org) and East Bay Children's Book Project (www.eastbaychildrensbookproject.org)—Provide books to families and programs in the San Francisco Bay area.
- Book Fairies (https://thebookfairies.org)—Provides books to families and programs throughout metropolitan New York.
- Reach Out and Read (https://reachoutandread.org)—National program that provides books to programs.
- First Book (https://firstbook.org)—National program that provides donations or low-cost books to programs to share with families.
- Lisa Libraries (http://lisalibraries.org)—Program that provides books to programs to share with families.

Book Sharing Programs

- Raising a Reader (www.raisingareader.org)—Book bag rotation program.
- Tandem Partners in Early Learning (www.tandembayarea.org)—Book bag rotation program.

References

American Academy of Pediatrics. (2021). Where we stand: Screen time. Retrieved from www.hea lthychildren.org/English/family-life/Media/Pages/Where-We-Stand-TV-Viewing-Time.aspx.

Arena, J., & Gomez, B. (2014). *Besos for baby*. Little, Brown Books for Young Readers.

Babin, S., & Roode, D. (2018). *Where are you, teddy?* Twirl/Editions Milan.

Bauer, M., & Katz, K. (2003). *Toes, ears, and nose*. Simon and Schuster.

Birckmayer, J., Kennedy, A., & Stonehouse, A. (2008). *From lullabies to literature: stories in the lives of infants and toddlers*. National Association for the Education of Young Children.

Bowey, C. W., & Willingham, B. (2000). *Busy toes*. Charlesbridge.

Boynton, S. (2017). *Barnyard dance*. Seedlings.

Carle, E., & Martin, B. (1997). *Brown bear, brown bear, what do you see?* Puffin.

Hughes, K. (2009). How social stories support the literacy learning of young toddlers. In D. Meier (Ed.), *Here's the story: Using narrative to promote children's language and literacy learning* (pp. 63–70). Teachers College Press.

Joosse, B. M., & Lavallee, B. (1991). *Mama, do you love me?* Chronicle Books.

Keats, E. J. (1962). *The snowy day*. Puffin Books.

Lin, G. (2001). *Dim sum for everyone!* Alfred A. Knopf.

Mangione, P., & Greenwald, D. (Eds.). (2011). *Infant/toddler caregiving: A guide to language development and communication* (2nd ed.). California Department of Education.

Mora, P. (2008). *Let's eat! ¡A comer!* HarperCollins Publishers.

Morales, Y. (2018). *Dreamers*. Neal Porter Books.

National Center for Family Literacy. (2021). Tips for parents: Choosing books for infants and toddlers. Retrieved from https://eclkc.ohs.acf.hhs.gov/parenting/article/tips-parents-choosing-books-infants-toddlers.

Schickedanz, J. A. (1999). *Much more than the ABCs: The early stages of reading and writing*. National Association for the Education of Young Children.

Schickedanz, J., & Collins, M. (2013). *So much more than the ABCs*. National Association for the Education of Young Children.

Tsong, J. J. (2013). *Twinkle, twinkle small hoku*. Beach House Publishing.

12 Supporting Children's Creative and Artistic Expression from Multiple Perspectives

Haneefah Shuaibe-Peters

Opening Reflections

1 What is the role of artistic and creative exploration in your overall philosophy of language and literacy education for infants and toddlers?
2 What specific strategies and approaches do you use, or would like to use, to promote young children's artistic and creative exploration?
3 How do you support access to open-ended sensory exploration and artistic experimentation for all children, even if their creative process is "messy" and may not fit your idea of what art should look like?

Introduction

In this chapter, I provide parents, teachers, and administrators with ideas and strategies for the successful development of infants' and toddlers' artistic and creative expression and imagination. The strategies that I discuss all depend on our embodied belief that infants are born with infinite potential and capacity for artistic and creative expression at every stage of their development. Although my ideas and strategies are relatively simple to implement, they do require a high level of consciousness and awareness of the needs of infants and toddlers at their various stages of artistic and creative development (Gardner, 1982; Korn-Bursztyn, 2012; Wright, 2015). The strategies that I discuss in this chapter align with infancy's three stages of development: young, mobile, and older (Lally et al., 1990). For each stage, I share my views and strategies on how artistic and creative expression can be approached and supported by parents, providers/teachers, and administrators of infant-toddler programs.

My Roles—Parent, Provider, and Administrator

I am an African American woman born and raised in the San Francisco Bay Area. I'm married with three African American children, two boys and a girl, and early childhood education has been my only professional passion. Becoming a mother was a significant cornerstone in my overall journey as an early learning professional. Each of my children arrived at notable periods in my career development and influenced my knowledge of their artistic learning in the areas of language and literacy in different ways. When my first son was born, I was just beginning my child development studies, yet eager to apply all of my theoretical learning to my parenting practices. I call this "the parent" phase of my career. I subsequently learned how to apply theories of artistic and language development to my practice, which enlightened and structured my early parenting experiences.

DOI: 10.4324/9781003227816-17

My second son arrived 5 years later, and his birth came with developmental concerns. Fortunately, through my training and education, I felt confident and equipped to support him on his developmental journey. In this "provider" or teacher stage of my career path, it was my son who taught me how to deepen my artistic and language intentionality and skills in working with young children. Five years later, my daughter was born at a point when I was fairly an established and knowledgeable early childhood professional. I call this "the administrator" stage of my journey. She taught me the importance of developing a mindset for navigating a holistic approach to children's artistic language and literacy learning. This navigation process requires critical thinking as I refine and reconsider how best to apply my knowledge of young children's development in ways that are tailored to each child's unique needs.

In all three of my roles and perspectives, I advocate for freedom of expression and creativity for my children and other young children of Color. I have always believed in educators not putting my children "into a box of what they can and can't do as African American children. I want them to have original thoughts and to think beyond what is in front of them" (Meier, 2020, p. 34).

The Parent: Setting the Foundation for Artistic Expression in the Young Infant

As a mother, my general philosophy is that until children are three years old, let them express themselves artistically however they like as long as it is safe. This is the foundation for creativity and artistic expression. As Kadir Nelson notes:

> As we consider the present moment, I feel more than ever that no time is better suited for using our creativity to spread and make something beautiful and share it with the world, a practice I learned from my mother at an early age.
>
> (Nelson, 2020, p. 2)

The fundamental goal for young infants (0–8 months) is to figure out the needs of their own bodies while also determining who will support the requisite secure feelings and environmental conditions. A young infant's vulnerability is part of their early journey, and as parents we provide the security that the young infant desires. As parents, we focus on meeting the young infant's needs both emotionally and physically. When done well and with intention, infants' early social and emotional experiences are foundational for the development of their future artistic and creative expressions. This foundation comes from young infants having experiences that help them learn about and strengthen their ability to manage sensory inputs.

When we support healthy sensory integration skills for infants and toddlers, they are more likely to engage in current and future creative and artistic expression. The roots of their artistic expression involve taking what is known and creating something new and original. In young infancy, we can focus on supporting children to make the known a deeply pleasurable and trusting experience. In this way, children learn to engage in sensorial experiences with confidence, elevating their cognitive ability to see beyond what is currently known. The stronger children's sensorial awareness, the better equipped they are for exploration that leads to varied forms of artistic expression and expanding their imagination. Furthermore, as infants develop within secure and protective environments, their desire for exploration grows from knowing that these protections remain constant. For infants especially, every moment is a new intense sensory experience, and it is our challenge to create sensory environments that are stimulating, but not overwhelming. We achieve this balance not by overprotecting children from sensory experiences, but rather from gradually introducing new sensory input so that infants can successfully integrate these experiences into their daily lives.

> ### Key Idea
>
> We achieve this balance not by overprotecting children from sensory experiences, but rather from gradually introducing new sensory input so that infants can successfully integrate these experiences into their daily lives.

It is helpful, then, for parents to be reflective of the benefits and challenges to children's sensory exposure. For instance, is the space for infants too loud or too quiet, bright or dark? Is the air fresh, temperature tolerable? Are the smells pleasurable? Are we protecting infants from feelings of pain or discomfort?

Since I have been an early childhood practitioner longer than I have been a parent, my parenting practices have been deeply influenced by my experiences and learning in the field. I have always wanted to allow my children to have freedom of expression with artistic materials. I never let "development" be a factor in the materials I allow my children to use, or in the ways that my children use these materials. For example, under my supervision and guidance, I have allowed my children at the age of 18 months to use child-sized scissors. I have found that exposure to creative materials broadened and deepened my children's skills beyond traditional developmental expectations. For instance, none of my children ever held writing materials with an open palm; rather, I helped them to control writing tools such as markers and pencils with a conventional "pencil grip," three-finger grasp.

Further, as an African American parent, I don't want my children held back by any erroneous expectations that children of Color only need structured, skills-based teaching. I don't want them to be "invisible" to teachers in their language and artistic development (Meier, 2020, p. 35). They deserve to be exposed to the full range of open-ended, creative and artistic learning, and to learn how to manipulate a healthy range of artistic tools and techniques.

> ### Key Idea
>
> Educators must recognize and make visible the desire for sensory exploration and the artistic talents and strengths of African American and other children of Color.

The Provider: Establishing Environments for Mobile Infants to Learn Artistic Expression

Once children grow into mobile infancy (6–18 months) they begin to demonstrate their innate desire to explore and express themselves physically. As I observe young children at this stage, I can decode what they are trying to communicate through their scribbling, painting, and other creative actions (Gandini, 2005). In my role as provider, I also use my observations of children at this stage to create environments that support children's ongoing artistic and creative growth and development. An engaging and intriguing environment nurtures the mobile infant's growing artistic abilities and interests. An effective artistic environment must have few limitations; to be creative and artistically expressive, one primarily needs freedom.

Key Idea

An effective artistic environment has few limitations; to be creative and artistically expressive, one primarily needs freedom.

Though as providers we must keep safety in mind, we also must learn to trust that secure mobile infants have the capacity to keep themselves safe. Mobile infants only gain a sense of confidence in their actions from providers who demonstrate their desire to protect children from harm during this vulnerable stage of infancy and young toddlerhood. Children who are securely attached often show a capacity and determination to navigate potentially hazardous or dangerous situations or objects as they ask themselves, "What would my provider say if they saw me with this or doing this?" Securely attached mobile infants learn to use data to navigate independent situations safely, but they need freedom to do so. As mobile infants, their curiosity fuels their appetite for learning, and the level of freedom they are afforded influences the depth of their artistic exploration and creative thinking.

Mobile infancy is all about experimentation as children utilize knowledge gained from their sensory experiences in young infancy, and apply that knowledge to objects and humans to create an expanding repertoire of meaning- and symbol-making tools. Natural environments allow mobile infants to bring these elements together, and to begin to learn the laws of creation, as creation is the ultimate artist. Thoughtfully designed natural environments provide mobile infants with artistic information, colors, sounds, textures, functions, and rules of physics. Developing the mobile infants' understanding of the natural environment creates space for creativity for imaginative creations yet to be discovered.

As both a parent and provider, I support young children's curiosity for exploration by building confidence through artistic expression. Young children need confidence to experiment with objects and materials in artistically and aesthetically pleasing ways. This confidence primarily comes from secure attachments to parents and other caregivers and family and community settings. Sensory experiences are a powerful channel for such confidence-building for young children, as they allow children to express themselves and show pride and a sense of achievement in their creations. When children have a strong sense of security, they share their joy with their providers who in turn can express their own sense of joy in the beauty of children's artistic processes and products. When children take the initiative to share their artistic expression with adults, as well as older siblings and other children, their invitations for sharing indicate feelings of "look what I have done" or "do you want to join me?"

When young children know that caring providers and others will respond to their invitations for sharing, and also give them the freedom to experiment with varied materials at their own pace, children gauge their own levels of safety in the activity. Children experiment and create while simultaneously watching and waiting for adults to set a limit, essentially asking, "Are you going to stop me?" So it is critical for providers to create artistic activities that children see as "limitless" as possible. When we provide structured and yet open-ended parameters for children's artistic expression, this provides a foundation for confidence building for young children who can say to themselves, "When I am expressing myself creatively, I can do so much without boundaries."

The Administrator: Developing an Educator's Mindset to Supporting Artistic Behaviors

As an administrator, I provide direct support for providers/teachers and indirect scaffolding for the children. It is essential for administrators to develop a level of trust with providers to strengthen our collective identities as agents of creative and artistic change. Having a clearly established mindset of artistic action also helps us approach our work with infants and toddlers as thoughtful and collaborative creators, innovators, and artists.

> **Key Idea**
>
> Having a clearly established mindset of artistic action also helps us approach our work with infants and toddlers as thoughtful and collaborative creators, innovators, and artists.

As mobile infants transition into older toddlerhood (16–36 months) their dominant concern becomes identity development. The use of expressive language emerges within typically developing children at this age, and providers must live by a mindset of older infants as deeply capable of communicating their true needs through language and other expressive means. Older toddlers gain a new sense of security to become confident explorers, ready to define and identify themselves as such, and to learn what they like and dislike and why. Artistic expression is an excellent space for them to work through these feelings, and older toddlers thrive on a range of developmentally appropriate art materials for scribbling and mark-making (Baghban, 2007; Dunst & Gorman, 2009; Meier, 2000). When children at this stage engage in artistic expression, providers can withhold deep opinions of their artistic creations, and engage children in conversations about their creative thinking and process. The overall goal is to help children identify with their creation, rather than feeling validated solely by providers' opinions of the creation. It is effective, then, to observe and reflect on what children enjoy about the materials and process, which in turn supports children to become more reflective about the use of artistic materials to advance their creative processes.

As an administrator of infant-toddler programs, I encourage my teaching staff to present children with artistic, sensory-driven experiences that encourage curiosity and a beginning level of cognitive distance and artistic problem-solving. This challenges children's cognition and confidence. In such circumstances, children either seek support from a trusted adult or engage more deeply as a way to resolve the cognitive dissonance, and either decision ultimately results in learning something new. So I work with teachers to create safe spaces for children to freely explore with materials, and I discourage providers from using the terms "mess" and "messy" when discussing exploration (or its aftermath) of an art or creative activity or project. These terms detract from the creative and artistic importance of what children have just organically expressed. I find it valuable to support an artistic approach, for instance, where paint on children's hands and clothes and on other "non-art" objects represents culturally responsive (Alanís & Iruka, 2021) and developmentally appropriate learning (National Association for the Education of Young Children, 2022). When we move beyond both individual and collective fear of the "messy art" factor, children sense an increased freedom for enjoyment, flow, and calm in their art play and creation (Figures 12.1 and 12.2).

The term "messy" diminishes the importance of what children have just organically expressed, or are in the midst of creating—infants and toddlers are almost always in-

Figure 12.1 Child examines his hands as he hand paints

Figure 12.2 Child presses both of his hands in the paint

Table 12.1 Parent, provider, and administrator roles in promoting infant-toddler artistic expression

Stage	Parent	Teacher/Provider	Leader/Administrator
Young infant (0–8 months)	• View the world through infants' senses • Acknowledge how we as adults have normalized our sensory experiences • Provide opportunities for children to get to know their body and its different functions • Limit child's feelings of being stressed and overwhelmed	• Take inventory of the classroom environment for access to art materials • Arrange everything to benefit children's needs • Make sure the sensory stimulations are not overwhelming • Understand one's pedagogical stance promotes deep learning	• Support teachers' development of a mindset for seeing infants and toddlers' artistic and creative capabilities through a lens of deep respect • Model this way of being with infants and toddlers alongside teachers
Mobile infant (6–18 months)	• Respect children's desires to explore and move within their environments • Provide different colors, textures, and natural smells • Take children directly to objects and discuss their characteristics • Be present in the children's explorative play • Intervene only when the child needs support • Communicate your presence: "I'm fully here if you need me, but I trust that you can explore safely"	• Promote a "yes" environment • Allow child to climb and touch objects in space • Remove safety concerns to allow for focused observations • Create art activities that engage child's senses through colors and textures • Expect child to place objects in their mouth as further sensory exploration and soothing • Allow children to play with their food	• Nurture the mindset that children are artists at work • Support teachers to encourage children's free exploration of environments and materials • Support teachers to not approach children's exploration from a place of fear • Help teachers see children as fully capable of caring for and artistically expressing themselves
Older infant (16–36 months)	• Encourage problem-solving skills during artistic exploration • Respect children's process of understanding what they like/dislike and how they communicate their opinions • Practice patience if art projects become "messy" • Recognize that limits help a child define their likes and dislikes • Understand how limit setting can promote children's sense of security • Present older infants with choices in the form of objects and behaviors	• Create art environments for the child to express what they are newly capable of doing • Create art routines and activities that allow them to practice self-help skills • Support language during activities • Offer children full control of their art experiences • Let children "finish" when they move away from an activity • Talk about their art without praising the creation • Display art in defined spaces to convey that children's art brings value to the space	• Provide professional development on honoring children's art as an integral part of their language and communicative competence • Help teachers avoid the impulse to praise children's art; discuss the process instead • Provide ongoing opportunities for collaborative inquiry, documentation, and reflection on children's artistic development and teachers' guidance

process in their evolving artistic interests and talents. Cleanliness should be the least of our concerns when we provide children with artistic choices for activities and projects. Our collaborative focus as administrators, providers, and families must remain in the space of "what opportunity can we create for children to strengthen their sensory talents and interests while also learning new information about the materials and how they can be used?" This effort also includes an awareness of children's levels of sensory tolerance as well as their growing repertoire of preferences for artistic tools, materials, media, representation, and sharing. I collaborate with teachers so that we have an ever-expanding toolbox of documentation, inquiry, and reflection tools for observing children during artistic expression, and together we dialogue about how and why we can further children's artistic development. A key ingredient for effective arts education administration for infants and toddlers is predicated on a deep and broad knowledge base of the role of varied adults for supporting children's artistic expression (Table 12.1).

While these roles may not apply to every educator and family member, they do offer a comprehensive picture of how all adults involved in children's lives can collectively promote children's artistic and creative development.

Closing Thoughts

There are infinite ways to support infant and toddlers' artistic and creative abilities. The ideas and strategies that I have presented in this chapter are tools to help us scaffold young children's creative and artistic development in a range of educational settings. Each stage of young children's development must be respected as distinctly separate, and yet the stages are undeniably intertwined as children grow and learn to express themselves. Infants and toddlers crave learning; they naturally seek their own paths of development and their growth patterns unfurl to help them meet their evolving desires. Young infants need a sense of safety, mobile infants need a secure environment for experimentation and exploration, and older infants appreciate opportunities to express their experiences and define who they are. As infants and toddlers use their biological, natural, and cultural desires to create and express themselves in creative and artistic ways, we must strengthen their navigation tools while also adjusting their environments and experiences accordingly.

Closing Reflections

1   In looking again at Table 12.1, how does Haneefah's description of the parent, provider, and administrator roles deepen your knowledge base for guiding infant-toddler artistic and creative self-expression?

2   How might you put into practice some of Haneefah's ideas for promoting messy art while refraining from praising children's artistic creations? How might you also explain this approach to families?

3   How might you observe infants and toddlers during their sensory play and artistic exploration, and support connections between their artistic processes and products?

References

Alanís, I., & Iruku, I. U. (Eds.). (2021). *Advancing equity & embracing diversity in early childhood education: Elevating voices*. National Association for the Education of Young Children.

Baghban, M. (2007). Scribbles, labels, and stories: The role of drawing in the development of writing. *Young Children*, 62(1), 20–26.

Dunst, C., & Gorman, E. (2009). Development of infant and toddler mark making and scribbling. *Centre for Early Learning Literacy Review, 2*(1), 1–16.

Gandini, L. (Ed.). (2005). *In the spirit of the studio: Learning from the atelier of Reggio Emilia.* Teachers College Press.

Gardner, H. (1982). *Artful scribbles: The significance of children's drawings.* Basic Books.

Korn-Bursztyn, C. (Ed.). (2012). *Young children and the arts: Nurturing imagination and creativity.* Information Age Publishing.

Lally, J. R. (Executive Producer/Content Developer/Writer), Mangione, P. L. (Content Developer/Writer), Signer, S. (Content Developer/Writer), & Butterfield, G. O. (Editor). (1990). *The ages of infancy: Caring for young, mobile, and older infants* [DVD]. California Department of Education.

Meier, D. R. (2000). *Scribble scrabble: Learning to read and write—Success with diverse teachers, children, and families.* Teachers College Press.

Meier, D. R. (2020). *Supporting literacy for children of color—A strength-based approach to preschool literacy.* Routledge.

National Association for the Education of Young Children. (2022). *Developmentally appropriate practice in early childhood programs: Serving children from birth through age 8.* National Association for the Education of Young Children.

Nelson, K. (2020). Read Kadir Nelson's 2020 Coretta Scott King Book Award illustrator acceptance speech at ALA's virtual book award celebration. Retrieved from www.hbook.com/story/2020-csk-illustrator-award-acceptance-by-kadir-nelson.

Wright, S. (2015). *Children, meaning-making and the arts.* Pearson.

Index